I0062838

Between
Flights

Between Flights

Reflections on the Unspoken Truths of Leadership and Life

Wendy Walker

GRAMMAR
FACTORY
— EST⁰ 2013 —

Between Flights
Copyright © 2025 by Wendy Walker.
All rights reserved.

Published by Grammar Factory Publishing, an imprint of MacMillan
Company Limited.

No part of this book may be used or reproduced in any manner what-
soever without the prior written permission of the author, except
in the case of brief passages quoted in a book review or article. All
enquiries should be made to the author.

Grammar Factory Publishing
MacMillan Company Limited
25 Telegram Mews, 39th Floor, Suite 3906
Toronto, Ontario, Canada
M5V 3Z1

Walker, Wendy.
Between Flights: Reflections on the Unspoken Truths
of Leadership and Life / Wendy Walker.

Paperback ISBN 978-1-998528-74-5
eBook ISBN 978-1-998528-75-2
Audiobook ISBN 978-1-998528-83-7

1. BUS071000 BUSINESS & ECONOMICS / Leadership.
2. BUS085000 BUSINESS & ECONOMICS / Women in Business.
3. SEL027000 SELF-HELP / Personal Growth / Success

Production Credits
Cover design by Designerbility
Interior layout design by Setareh Ashrafologhalai
Book production and editorial services by Grammar Factory
Publishing

Grammar Factory's Carbon Neutral Publishing Commitment
Grammar Factory Publishing is proud to be neutralizing the carbon
footprint of all printed copies of its authors' books printed by or
ordered directly through Grammar Factory or its affiliated companies
through the purchase of Gold Standard-Certified International Offsets.

Disclaimer
The material in this publication is of the nature of general comment
only and does not represent professional advice. It is not intended
to provide specific guidance for particular circumstances, and it
should not be relied on as the basis for any decision to take action
or not take action on any matter which it covers. Readers should
obtain professional advice where appropriate, before making any
such decision. To the maximum extent permitted by law, the author
and publisher disclaim all responsibility and liability to any person,
arising directly or indirectly from any person taking or not taking
action based on the information in this publication.

*For my Dad, who unknowingly shaped
the path I chose, and for my Son, who
gives me the reason to keep walking it.*

Contents

How It
All Started

'M SO GRATEFUL you're here, reading this. Time is the one thing none of us can multiply, so the fact that you've chosen to spend time with me is something I don't take lightly.

You may be wondering—where did this book come from?

During the last couple of years, I have spent more hours than I can count in airports and on flights. After a while, I was travelling so much for work that I couldn't bring myself to watch another inflight movie. Instead, I found myself staring out the window or sitting in silence with nothing but my own thoughts for company.

I've always been good at that, sitting with my own thoughts. Maybe it comes from being raised much like an only child, with two much older brothers. I learnt early how to keep myself occupied and turn silent thoughts into adventures and stories. On these flights, and in between them, that habit returned. While the world rushed around me, I started to notice what was happening beneath the surface of my own life: the exhaustion, the joy, the questions that lingered.

On one late-night flight back from Sydney, I was balancing a tray table full of cold airline food and scrolling through emails when a text from my son popped up: '*Did you land yet? Goodnight Mum.*' I felt the sting of tears; guilt for not being there, relief that he still reached for me and the ache of knowing I was running on empty. That was when I opened the Notes app on my phone and typed a single sentence: *This pace isn't sustainable.*

That sentence became the seed of these reflections. I began to use the in-between times to reflect on what was happening and how I was feeling, and try to make some sense of it.

I wasn't thinking about publishing my reflections, or even having other people read them. These were just fragments; small reflections on what it means to lead, to juggle, to keep showing up. But over time, they started to add up and be added to, and finally a friend convinced me that these reflections were something I should shape and share.

I have spent more than twenty-five years leading teams across industries and geographies, often while juggling life as a single mum, and I did not write these reflections as an observer. They were born from the real tension of trying to do it all: building careers and companies while also building a life. Many of the insights in this book are drawn from my personal experiences, but others come from the wisdom of peers and senior leaders I've had the privilege to walk alongside. What they share is that they are not theory—they are lived experience.

This book is a collection of those reflections. They're not intended to be instructions or a leadership playbook. They're drawn from honest moments found in the in-between times when I was tired, or hopeful, or wrestling with the complexity of leading both a career and a life.

Inside these pages, you'll find my thoughts on themes that don't get much airtime: the unseen labour, the invisible weight leaders carry, the emotional nuance behind decisions, and the balance between ambition and grace. These are not always the themes that make headlines, but they're the ones that follow us home and keep us awake.

You can read the reflections in the order they appear, if you want to, or you can pick one that fits where you are today, put the book down, then pick it up again another day. You might find a reflection that speaks to you today and another that makes sense six months from now. That's the beauty of reflections: they arrive when you need them. Each stands alone, but together they offer a fuller picture of what it feels like to lead and to live in the thick of it.

My hope is simple. That these pages give you a pause, the way they gave me one. A chance to see your own leadership and your own juggle a little differently. To feel less alone in it all, and to remember that even in the noise, the work you're doing matters.

Leadership isn't neat. It's rarely balanced. But it's real. And sometimes, it's in the silence between flights that what really matters finally lands.

1

The Juggle
Is Real

USED TO CHASE balance like it was a destination; a finish line I could reach if I just worked harder. But it's more like jazz: unpredictable, improvised and sometimes off-key, but always moving.

The reality is that my days rarely follow a predictable rhythm. In fact, most of the time the juggle feels less like jazz and more like drowning.

Let me tell you about one memorable day. My alarm went off at 5:30 a.m., I scrambled eggs while reciting reminders about forgotten homework, raced through a quick shower, dialled into a quarterly numbers call with hair still dripping, dashed into the office, sat through six back-to-back meetings that stretched to five hours without a break, then sprinted to the rugby sidelines to support my son—where I realised I'd eaten nothing that day.

That night, I stirred pasta for dinner with one hand while I answered emails with the other. At midnight, I climbed into bed, laptop still warm, inbox finally at zero. I closed my eyes and thought, 'And tomorrow, I'll do it all again.'

It's messy, unscripted and relentless. And that's the real rhythm of the juggle. A rhythm built from playing too many roles in a single day—professional, leader, coach, mother—and sometimes switching between all of them in a single hour.

Juggling all this doesn't leave much white space on the calendar, and I'm often asked how I do it. The reality is I don't always. I'm human—I drop balls now and then, I say no sometimes and occasionally I go to bed with unanswered emails.

But the relentless pace isn't just mine. I see it everywhere. Many incredible people I know are navigating similar paths; juggling leadership, life and the daily grind. There's the colleague managing a global role while caring for an ageing parent. A friend juggling a start-up with a newborn who wakes every three hours. Leaders who look calm on the outside, but are carrying invisible loads that never make it onto a calendar.

It's not easy. It can be exhausting. And everyone's version of the juggle looks different. But what we do share is this relentless background hum: the pressure to keep all the pieces moving, all the time.

And the volume we're all carrying just keeps growing.

As I write this, I find myself asking: Why is this? Perhaps we haven't noticed how much external pressure has been added to the pace. Over the past decade, the bar for productivity has been steadily pushed upwards. The arrival of AI means more can be done in less time, and many organisations expect leaders and teams to keep accelerating in response.

At the same time, we're living in a very different era. The shift into and out of remote work during Covid changed how many of us thought about work and time.

For a while, working from home gave us a taste of what it was like to have more flexibility. We could power through household chores between work calls, enjoy a walk outside instead of a commute—some of us even felt more productive. But now, in a post-Covid world, the pendulum has swung the other way. Most of us are commuting to and from the office again, creating a longer day. Travel expectations have resumed and, for many, increased. For some, the flexibility of remote working is limited. And yet we're all being asked to keep our full performance across more contexts, more distractions, more transitions. All this adds more invisible weight, because we're not just juggling tasks—we're juggling shifting norms, heightened expectations, hybrid boundaries and technologies that help in some ways but also create more demand. It's no wonder it can feel like the juggle owns us, rather than the other way around.

What I've learnt, especially this year, is that presence is the real metric. Not perfection. Giving the right version of myself, fully, in each moment and in each role I play, and compartmentalising with care, helps to ground me. And I believe this leads to better outcomes. If I can be fully present in the moment, whether I'm leading a meeting, answering a late-night WhatsApp from a friend or sitting at the kitchen table with my son while he studies, I count that as success. Because when I'm present—not just physically, but mentally and emotionally—everything runs a little smoother. Not perfectly, but with more clarity.

It's not about strict boundaries; they don't always hold. It's about creating enough space, even just mentally, to fully be where I am.

Let's come back to the jazz metaphor. Balance isn't found in hitting every note and filling every beat. It's in knowing when to stop, pause and say no. When to stretch yourself, when to go with the flow, and when to give yourself space. Leadership and life rarely play out in perfect harmony. It's messy. It's human. And for me, it's real.

That's why in-between moments matter. Not because they resolve the chaos, but because they soften it.

For me, the space during travel became a place to pause, to make sense of the pace, to recalibrate and to then carry on with grace.

These moments also allowed me to create room to write honestly about the things we don't always say out loud: the exhaustion, the doubt, the joy, the stretch. And somehow, by giving shape to this load, it became lighter to carry.

Wherever you are—navigating the noise, moving through the motions or sitting in a rare moment of stillness—I hope this reflection has presented a moment for your own thoughts to land, and for you to identify where your in-between is. Because sometimes the most meaningful insights don't arrive in the rush, but in the pause. And maybe, just maybe, the juggle doesn't need to be perfectly balanced; just consciously held.

So I invite you to consider:

- What roles are you juggling most right now?
- Which role is being neglected?
- What would presence look like in just one of those roles tomorrow?
- Where can you make time for your in-between?
- And what might you find there that can help you be present with what matters most for you?

2

Your Personal Boardroom

M Y REFLECTIONS OFTEN begin in the in-between and the quiet gaps; the moments in an empty boardroom between meetings, in my car driving to the next appointment or sitting in an aircraft on the tarmac, waiting patiently for a delayed flight to take off. These moments force me to catch my breath and let an idea settle.

It was a simple shared moment, however, that sparked this reflection. I was mid-conversation, halfway through a sentence, and someone I trust interrupted, gently but firmly, and said, 'That's not the real question, is it?'

My stomach flipped. I laughed awkwardly to buy time. But I knew they were right.

I remember gripping my coffee cup, heat seeping into my palm, as silence stretched longer than felt safe. My instinct was to defend myself, to keep performing. Instead, I exhaled and admitted: 'No, it isn't.' That moment forced me to acknowledge something that I knew but perhaps wasn't ready to address. And it reminded me how important it is to have people in your life who don't just nod along, but help you dig deeper, think sharper and stay true to yourself.

I felt that intensely during the pandemic. When life slowed and the noise fell away, we all sharpened our awareness of who really mattered. The people who checked in for no reason. Who took time for us. Who reminded us of who we were, even when we weren't quite sure ourselves. The ones who didn't need a calendar invite to show up. Sometimes it was a childhood friend who sent a text just because they thought of you, a colleague who took five minutes to ask how you really are, or a family member who showed up at the door without being asked.

As the pace of life today keeps accelerating, I worry we're losing that clarity. That we're drifting away from some of the truths we uncovered when the things that didn't matter fell away. The insight that connection is not about volume; it's about depth.

That's why I've come to value, more than ever, what I call my personal boardroom.

It's not a formal advisory board. Not a LinkedIn network. It's a small circle of people who play very different roles in my life, often without realising it. They are the voices I return to when I need clarity, the mirrors that reflect truths I can't always see, and the anchors who keep me steady when life is moving fast. Together they shape my thinking, challenge my assumptions and remind me of who I am.

There's the one who always tells me the truth, even when it's hard to hear. They're my compass; my reality check when I start to drift. One industry colleague once asked me, 'Why do you keep yourself so busy? Is it a coping mechanism?' Until that moment I had never realised that, in fact, it was. And having it named out loud forced me to pause and look at what I'd been avoiding.

Or the person who sparks my creativity when I'm stuck in spreadsheets. They bring energy, colour and possibility— especially when I can't see it myself.

Another advocates for me in rooms I'm not in. This person's belief in me has opened more doors than they probably realise, and given me confidence to take steps I may never have taken without that belief. And I've heard the same from others. One leader told me about an advocate who, unexpectedly, put her forward for a board role she never imagined she'd be considered for. That single act changed the trajectory of her career.

Then there's the one who reminds me to rest. Who doesn't measure my worth by output or job title, and who gently slows me down when I need it most. Sometimes it's as simple as, 'Come over, we'll watch our favourite movie again.'

Or the friend who makes me laugh when I take it all too seriously. A necessary reminder that lightness is not the opposite of leadership; it's part of it.

And the one who simply reminds me that I am enough, just as I am. No embellishment needed. No performance required. A close friend often reminds me that I'm doing a wonderful job raising my son. For anyone raising a child and carrying a heavier load than you thought you could, you'll understand how that simple reminder allows me to exhale and know that sometimes just being present is enough.

These people don't always know when they're playing their part. But I do. And in days and weeks when I'm carrying a lot, this boardroom is essential.

While I describe my own boardroom in terms of the roles people play in my life, the idea itself isn't new. There's a framework that can be a helpful way to think about it, which lists twelve different roles that tend to fall into three groups.

- **Information roles**: people like the customer voice, the expert, the navigator or the inspirer. These are the people who bring you fresh insight or perspective or spark an idea when you're stuck.

- **Power roles**: the un-locker, the sponsor, the influencer or the connector. These are the people who create access, open doors, advocate for you in rooms you're not in or connect you to opportunities you might not find on your own.

- **Development roles**: the improver, the challenger, the nerve-giver or the anchor. These are the ones who stretch you, keep you grounded and remind you that you're human first.

And isn't it a gift to think that we could have people like this in our lives? To pause for a moment and recognise that many of us already do. When you read those descriptions, you might be able to picture the friend who always gives you the unfiltered truth, the colleague who champions you when you're not in the room or the family member who will just hug you and make you feel secure when everything else feels unsteady.

You don't need to fill all twelve roles—most of us never will—but thinking about it this way can change how you see the people in your life in their entirety. It's not about 'Who do

I know?' so much as 'Who helps me grow, who helps me move and who helps me stay grounded?' The more intentional you are, the stronger and more balanced your boardroom becomes.

And just like any real board, it shifts as you do. The roles you lean on when you're building your career may be different from the ones you need when you're leading a team, launching something new or dealing with the heavier parts of life. Having even a few of these people in your corner is something to cherish.

Leadership isn't just strategy and scale, it's also about staying human. Staying connected to people who see the full version of you—the one behind the job title. The people who ask, 'How are you, really?' and stay to hear the answer.

I'm deeply grateful for the people in my life who keep showing up—whether they challenge or support.

If you're juggling a lot right now, this could be your invitation to take stock of your personal boardroom.

So I invite you to consider:

- Who's at your table? Who do you need to call in closer? Who do you need to thank?

- Who are the people who really see you; not just your role, but your whole self?

- Who challenges you, encourages you, and reminds you of who you are when you forget?

- And how might you nurture those connections so they stay strong, even in the noise?

3

The Empathy Advantage

EMPATHY IS NOT often listed on a résumé. We talk about creativity, data, storytelling, commercial acumen and leadership. But empathy—the ability to truly see and understand others—is the subtle force that makes all those things work.

In marketing, we pride ourselves on understanding audiences. We study them, segment them, and build personas that capture their needs, motivations and pain points. We talk about customer-centricity as if it's our second language. But empathy goes deeper than that. It's not only about understanding customers, but also about understanding *people*.

While I write this from the perspective of a marketer, this applies across every profession. Whether you're in sales, finance, operations, law, design or education, empathy changes how you work. It determines how effectively you collaborate, how clearly you communicate and how closely you connect.

As a marketer, success depends on how well we can empathise—not only outwardly, but inwardly—across the business, with colleagues, teams, and even our critics. Because if we can't see the world through the eyes of the people we work with, our ideas will always fall short of their full potential.

Early in my career, I saw empathy mostly as a creative tool; something that helped me build campaigns that resonated emotionally. I learnt that behind every target audience was a real person with hopes, frustrations and needs. That shift was transformative. Campaigns that connected emotionally didn't just perform better, they built loyalty. But as my leadership scope grew, I realised empathy had a much larger role to play. It wasn't just about connecting brands to customers; it was about connecting people to each other inside organisations.

You can create the most brilliant strategy in the world, but if the sales team doesn't believe in it, it won't land. You can build an award-winning campaign, but if finance doesn't understand its value, it won't get funded again. You can inspire your team to reach new creative heights, but if the executive team sees marketing as a cost centre rather than a growth engine, your impact will always be limited.

Empathy became the bridge.

I first learnt that lesson in a tough quarterly review early in my leadership journey. The sales team was under immense pressure. Targets were aggressive, pipelines were soft and there was growing frustration that marketing wasn't delivering leads fast enough. I remember sitting in that meeting feeling defensive. Our campaigns were performing and the numbers were solid. But as I listened to the head of sales speak, something shifted. I realised he wasn't frustrated with marketing; he was scared. His team's bonuses, his credibility, his standing with the regional head—all of it was on the line. And because I had spent the early part of my career in sales myself—leading teams, chasing targets, feeling the same pressure and responsibility—I understood exactly what that fear felt like. That experience gave me a level of empathy that changed how I responded.

So instead of defending our work, I asked if I could sit in on his team's Monday sales meetings for a few weeks.

What I learnt changed everything. I saw how deals moved and stalled. I saw the emotional cycle salespeople went through every month: the optimism, the doubt, the grind. I noticed how small things—a single new lead or a promising conversation—could lift the entire room.

That experience gave me new language, new empathy and new credibility. When I came back to my own team, I reframed how we talked about our campaigns. We stopped saying, 'We've delivered 300 leads,' and started saying, 'We've opened twenty-seven new conversations that could turn into revenue this quarter.' We began aligning our metrics with theirs. That simple act of empathy changed the relationship completely. We were no longer two functions working in parallel; we were partners.

Empathy also reshaped how I saw finance. I worked with a Chief Financial Officer who was deeply sceptical about marketing. Every presentation felt like a cross-examination, and I'd leave the room feeling like I had to defend creativity itself. At first, I saw finance as the obstacle. But over time, I began to see what was really happening; he wasn't trying to block marketing, he was trying to understand it. His world was risk and precision. Mine was possibility and persuasion.

So, I started telling our story differently. Instead of talking about 'brand affinity', I began showing 'cost of familiarity'. That is, how trusted brands reduced customer acquisition costs and increased retention. I built a model linking campaign investment to pipeline velocity and showed that the return wasn't abstract; it was measurable. And something shifted. He began to see marketing not as a cost, but as an asset—something that created long-term equity.

The empathy went both ways. I also learnt to appreciate the discipline finance brought. It forced me to tighten my business cases, clarify assumptions and think like an investor. It wasn't creativity versus constraint; it was creativity sharpened by constraint.

Empathy also extended to teams that rarely make it into the marketing conversation. I remember a website rebuild where tension quickly grew between the marketing and IT teams. Marketing wanted agility, beautiful design and real-time updates. IT wanted security, stability and scalability. Both sides were right, and both felt misunderstood. After one particularly frustrating meeting, I asked the IT lead to walk me through what kept him awake at night. He told me about his metrics, security breaches and the pressure of maintaining systems across multiple countries and compliance zones. I could see the weight of responsibility on his shoulders. So we approached the project differently. Instead of pushing for every feature we wanted, we agreed on shared priorities: performance, scalability and user experience. We started bringing the IT lead into our creative reviews, and we joined theirs. The tone changed overnight.

It reminded me that empathy doesn't require agreement; it requires understanding. When people feel seen, they stop resisting and start collaborating.

I've learnt that empathy isn't just functional, it's personal. It's about remembering that behind every email, every comment in a meeting, every 'no' that frustrates you, is a human being navigating their own pressures, expectations and stories.

I once worked with a regional HR director who was incredibly direct, almost confrontational, in meetings. My first instinct was to keep my distance. But after a long coffee one afternoon, I discovered her story. She'd spent years trying to earn respect in male-dominated industries, where being assertive was the only way to be heard. That context changed everything. I began to see her not as difficult, but as determined. That conversation built a bridge that changed how we worked together and taught me that empathy often begins with curiosity.

The irony is that the higher we rise in leadership, the easier it is to lose empathy. Meetings become bigger, data becomes cleaner and our distance from the day-to-day grows. We start talking about 'functions', 'resources' and 'headcount' instead of people. The language of efficiency replaces the language of understanding.

But empathy is not a soft skill; it's a strategic one. It's what allows leaders to see context before jumping to conclusions, to interpret silence as insight, to notice fatigue in a team before it turns into burnout. When empathy disappears, organisations harden. People stop speaking up. Creativity shrinks. Alignment erodes. And performance—the thing everyone was trying to protect—inevitably suffers.

Empathy doesn't mean saying yes to everything. It doesn't mean lowering standards or absorbing everyone's stress. It means leading with awareness and knowing when to push, when to pause and how to see the bigger picture.

I worked with a creative director who had mastered that balance. During high-pressure pitch weeks, he'd walk through the studio late at night with takeaway coffees for the team. He wouldn't lecture about deadlines or ask for progress updates. He'd just sit, listen and remind people why the work mattered. The next morning, people would show up early, re-energised. Not because they were told to, but because they *wanted* to. His empathy didn't dilute performance; it fuelled it.

Empathy creates trust, and trust accelerates everything: decision-making, innovation, accountability. It's the foundation of psychological safety, which is what allows creativity to flourish in the first place. And while I write this from the perspective of a marketer, these principles hold true for anyone. Whether you work in finance, law, design, education, healthcare or engineering, empathy changes how you work. It transforms how you communicate, how you lead and how you're received. It reminds you that success in any discipline is about the mastery of connection.

The best professionals, in any field, are those who stay connected to the humanity behind the work. They listen before they speak. They adapt without losing authenticity. They see colleagues as partners. And in doing so, they build influence that doesn't come from title or authority, but from trust.

Empathy doesn't make you less commercial, less strategic or less results-driven. It makes you more credible. It deepens understanding, sharpens collaboration and strengthens leadership. It's what turns good work into great work, and colleagues into allies.

And in a world that moves as fast as ours, that might just be the most powerful advantage of all.

So I ask you to consider:

- When was the last time you paused to see a situation through someone else's eyes?

- How might empathy change the way you approach your next meeting, project or conversation?

- Which relationships in your professional world would benefit from being seen with a little more understanding?

- And how can you build empathy into your daily rhythm, not as a reaction, but as a practice?

4

The Soft Flight
of Ambition

AMBITION HAS ALWAYS been a complicated word for me. I've never seen myself as ambitious in the traditional sense. For years, I resisted using the word to describe myself, because my version didn't look like the one that was celebrated.

I wasn't chasing promotions or titles or climbing ladders for the sake of it. I just wanted to do good work, to be known for the value I brought and to see the people around me thrive. Helping my team grow, progress in their careers and be recognised for their achievements has always felt just as important as any personal milestone. I remember when someone I had managed applied for a more senior role and got it—the position they doubted they could secure. They told me they never would have tried without my belief in them. That moment meant as much as any title I've ever carried. And it's still one of my proudest moments.

For me, that's always been enough. I've never needed a new definition of ambition, just the clarity to stay true to it even as the world around me shifted. The drive to lead with purpose, to create meaningful impact and to show up with integrity has never wavered.

As my career progressed and leadership deepened, I began to recognise success in new dimensions. Not because my ambition changed, but because I started to value the moments that aren't seen as much as the ones that are. The mentoring conversations. The tough calls made behind closed doors. The kind of impact that doesn't always make headlines, but shapes culture, people and momentum.

For many of us, ambition no longer looks like a linear upwards sprint. Instead, it's about balance, about impact, about integrity.

I see it in the colleague who quietly takes time each week to mentor graduates, knowing their effort won't show up on any KPI but believing it's where leadership is built. I see it in one of my own team members who, even when told not to, will stay up late polishing work until it's perfect because that's how she shows her pride in contributing. These are not the loud wins, but they are ambition all the same.

It's the work that aligns with who we are. Relationships that fuel us. Impact that lasts beyond the quarter. Less of a sprint up the ladder, more of a steady walk that gives you time to notice what's around you.

This kind of ambition shows up in small but important ways: choosing to create room in a meeting for a softer voice to be heard; saying no to a project that doesn't align with your values, even if it looks impressive; or choosing family when the calendar says work. It's about owning the choices that line up with what you care about.

Yet I've also felt the sting of being underestimated. More than once, someone assumed I wasn't ambitious enough because I didn't fight for the biggest title in the room. Those moments forced me to own my definition with conviction and articulate what was important to me.

I also recognise that this version of ambition may not resonate with everyone. For some, ambition is about the climb: stepping into big titles, leading large teams and making bold, visible moves. And that kind of ambition is valid, too. I know many people with that ambition, and I admire them. I think of a former colleague who set their sights on the C-suite from day one. Every move they made—the extra projects they volunteered for, the international relocations they accepted, the networking dinners they never missed—was in service of that goal. And it worked. Today, they're leading a global function, and they wear that ambition with pride. There is courage in raising your hand. There is clarity in owning your goals. And there is pride in moving with direction.

The traditional playbook told us to measure ambition by speed, scale and spotlight. To move fast and aim high. But I've found that the deeper kind of ambition, the one that sustains you, is often slower and more deliberate. It listens before it acts and questions the rules before following them.

And I've seen the view of ambition shifting, especially generationally. Many Boomers and Gen X still talk about ambition as tenure and title. Millennials often seek meaning and flexibility. Gen Z is rewriting ambition altogether, measuring it not only in career progression but in alignment with personal values, mental health and social impact. None of these is right or wrong. They're simply different expressions of the same human drive to matter. It takes courage to say, 'This is enough for me,' even if it doesn't fit a slide or someone else's expectation. That is not a lack of ambition. That is leadership on your terms.

At its best, ambition feels like alignment, not obligation; like your voice, not an echo.

And maybe that's part of why I write these reflections. Maybe ambition, for me, is also about legacy—not in a grand or ego-driven way, but in the small hope that what I've learnt might help someone else navigate their path with a little more clarity. That's why I stay active in our broader community. That's why I mentor, share and speak. Because I care about the next generation of leaders. And because passing it all on—the hard-earned lessons, the real stories, the unpolished truths—feels like a form of ambition I can stand behind. This version of ambition may not fit the standard mould, but it feels right for me. It's okay if your dreams have changed. That's not failure; that's growth.

Whether you're climbing, deepening, shifting or pausing, the real work is in staying honest with yourself about why you're doing it. And giving yourself permission to change your mind as you grow.

So I invite you to consider:

- What does ambition look like for you now?
- Is what you're chasing truly yours, or inherited from someone else's version of success?
- What would change if you gave yourself permission to redefine it?

5

The Flight Path
of Confidence

ONFIDENCE IS OFTEN celebrated as a fixed trait; you either have it or you don't. But I've found it to be far more fluid. Some days I feel grounded, clear, certain. Other days I hesitate. I overthink. I wonder if I'm getting it right at all.

Confidence, for me, doesn't always walk into the room first. Sometimes it waits for clarity to arrive. Sometimes it arrives mid-conversation. And sometimes, its presence is subtle; just enough to keep showing up.

In leadership, we're expected to be decisive, composed, unwavering. But confidence often coexists with doubt. And that doesn't make you less capable. It just makes you human.

I was reminded of this during a recent one-on-one with a colleague. She asked how I managed to be calm and in control while she was feeling overwhelmed and anxious. I told her, quite honestly, that I was overwhelmed too. The sense of relief that emanated from her after I said that was palpable; just knowing she wasn't alone in how she felt lifted something heavy.

I shared with her that sometimes I make a decision and then replay my reasoning over and over in my head. Not the kind of decision you can undo quickly, but one that affects people, teams and direction. I'll lie awake, scanning through every angle I considered, wondering if I missed something, if I should have made a different call. But the next morning, I still need to walk into the room and own it. So, I try to steady myself with the knowledge that I made the best decision I could with the information I had at the time.

One simple moment of truth—admitting I was overwhelmed too—cracked open a more honest conversation, and reminded me how powerful it can be to say the thing we often keep to ourselves. Because the doubt doesn't disappear; it sits beside me. And so does the acknowledgement that leadership isn't about always being certain—it's about standing in the choice you've made, knowing you made it with care.

There aren't people who don't feel overwhelmed at times. And I don't think a lack of confidence makes us less effective. If anything, it's a sign of how deeply we care about what we contribute; not just to our teams or companies, but to the people and purpose behind the work, and to the people surrounding us in our personal lives. That wobble you feel isn't weakness. It can be the weight of wanting to do things well, with integrity and heart.

As a child, I often spent time on stage, appearing in musical or dance performances. And I can still remember that flutter of nerves in my belly right before stepping into the spotlight.

That feeling wasn't always comfortable, but I learnt to welcome it. Because it meant I was stretching. It meant I cared.

That early experience shaped something in me. It taught me that confidence isn't the absence of nerves; it's the ability to move with them. It's understanding that fear and excitement often sit side by side. And that pushing beyond your comfort zone brings learning and accomplishment you never thought possible.

It's easy to compare your internal uncertainty to someone else's external composure—especially in leadership, where confidence can be confused with charisma. But I've learnt that people who appear the most certain are often carrying secret doubts. They've just learnt to move with them, not perform past them.

Confidence can also be rebuilt in small, intentional ways. By finishing what you start. By learning something new— even if you don't master it. By asking the brave question in a meeting. By showing up to a conversation you could have avoided. Each act of showing up becomes a thread. And over time, those threads weave into something steady enough to hold you, even on the days when you don't feel it.

For me, one of those threads is writing. I didn't start these reflections because I felt confident; I started them because I needed somewhere to place my thoughts. And over time, the act of shaping words gave me greater confidence in my own opinions and perspectives. I've also seen this in others. A friend once told me she started keeping a small 'done list' beside her to-do list. Each tick was a thread, and when doubt crept in, she could look back and see proof of progress.

That simple act slowly rewired how she saw herself—not as someone floundering, but as someone moving forward.

Lessons like that have helped guide me as a leader. I don't need to feel confident all the time, but I do need to act with intention and stay anchored in purpose rather than certainty. I understand that confidence isn't a prerequisite for action. It's often the result of showing up anyway.

It's why I keep a few people close who remind me of my voice. It's why I take time to reflect on the impact of my work, not the perfection of it. And it's why I try to protect moments in my calendar to recalibrate, not just perform.

Sometimes, we lead best by modelling the truth of leadership. I've found that when I share my own moments of hesitation with my team, it deepens trust rather than diminishing it. It shows them that confidence isn't something you wait for—it's something you practise together.

Confidence isn't fixed or final. It shifts. It bends. It shows up differently, depending on the moment. And that's what makes it real. Confidence doesn't need to be perfect to be powerful. It just needs to keep me moving—one step, one moment, one choice at a time.

So I invite you to consider:

- Where are you waiting for confidence to arrive before you act?

- What might shift if you trusted your intention—even when certainty isn't present?

6

The Window
Seat Perspective

THERE'S SOMETHING about a window seat.

It offers a frame within the frame and a way to look out while sitting still. It doesn't change the flight path, but it does change how we experience it. Sometimes the view is cinematic: a golden sunrise, a patchwork of farmland, the curve of the coastline coming into view. Sometimes it's nothing but clouds. Either way, the window seat creates perspective.

And in leadership, perspective is something we rarely make time for but constantly need.

Most leaders I know are seated in the aisle seat. Accessible. In motion. Always moving to the next thing. Always ready to step in, help out, respond fast. That's what good leadership can look like. But that posture doesn't easily lend itself to reflection. To the broader view. To the small shifts in altitude that signal something important is changing.

I know a regional GM who schedules one full 'window day' each quarter: no meetings, no emails—just time spent revisiting past decisions and scanning for emerging patterns. She told me it's the only time she can actually 'see the system', not just the schedule. It's a small practice, but one that's kept her feeling more in touch with her view of the business as a whole. And because she takes this time to gain perspective, her team also benefits from her ability to cut through the clutter and provide clear strategic direction.

When you shift to the metaphorical window seat of business, you give yourself permission to zoom out and take in the system around you. You notice the patterns that repetition makes easy to miss. You consider what's happening beneath the surface, rather than reacting to what's most urgent. Perspective is the difference between turbulence and trajectory. Between asking, 'What now?' and asking, 'What next?' Between being reactive and being intentional.

This isn't about being removed from the work. Quite the opposite. It's about staying anchored in the purpose behind the work. It's about noticing when the calendar is full, but the progress is thin. When decisions are being made fast, but not well. When you've stopped asking the questions you used to ask, because everyone's just trying to keep up.

We need leaders who can spend time in the window seat. To see more than just the next deliverable. To see how it all connects. How the culture is absorbing change. How the strategy is landing. How the team is really doing.

Some of the most important leadership insights come from pulling back. You might notice that what's been praised as high performance is high exhaustion. That the bold new strategy is missing a critical voice. That a recurring tension is a values misalignment, not a communication issue. Or that a high-performer's disengagement is a sign of something bigger than burnout. These aren't things we spot when we're rushing between gates. They reveal themselves in the pause. In the altitude and low hum of cruising speed, when we finally have a chance to look out and pay attention.

And there's another gift that the window seat offers: scale.

At altitude, the noise softens. Things feel less personal and less overwhelming. The issue that ate up half your day feels smaller because you've regained perspective on its place in the larger picture. That's not detachment, that's wisdom. It's the kind of wisdom that helps you choose what really needs your voice and what doesn't. What deserves energy and what can be delegated, delayed or let go.

And it can remind you why you lead in the first place. Perhaps you feel proud when you watch a team member step up or step in to take care of business.

For many of us, 'why' we lead can drift. It doesn't disappear, but it does get buried under goals, metrics, stakeholder expectations and calendar invites. But from the window seat, we can see our 'why' clearly again. Often unprompted, and often in a sentence or image or feeling that rises uninvited and brings instant clarity. That's the moment perspective gives us. It's not always dramatic, but it's deeply useful.

Sometimes, we don't choose the window seat, but we're forced into it by circumstance. It could be illness, or a change in structure or role. When that happens, it can feel disorienting. Like being grounded and watching others move forward while you sit still. But even in these moments, something valuable is happening. Stillness does not mean stagnation. Observation is also action.

When we return to the aisle, we return with better sightlines. We have clarity that's strategic, but also human. We speak less, but say more. We listen differently. We sense earlier. We build culture more intentionally. Not because we've read a new framework, but because we've seen what's been happening all along.

I once had a C-suite leader confide in me that after a change in management, they found themselves sidelined from the very business they'd helped to build. They said that at first, it felt like exile and they were frustrated by watching decisions unfold from the outside. But after a few months, distance brought insight. They realised how differently they saw the organisation when they weren't inside the noise. They saw the culture gaps, the unspoken assumptions, the opportunities hiding in plain sight. When they eventually stepped back in, they led with greater empathy and clarity. That pause changed not just their view, but their leadership.

This is a call to look up and look out. To take the window seat perspective every now and then and remember that leadership isn't just about speed. It's about sight. And when you're willing to shift your seat, even briefly, you might be surprised by what becomes visible.

So I invite you to consider:

- What are you seeing more clearly now than you did six months ago?

- Where could distance offer insight, not detachment?

- What vantage point have you been avoiding, and what might change if you allowed yourself to see it?

7

Why We Do
What We Do

VERY NOW AND THEN, I find myself wondering why I do what I do; why I made the choices I've made, and how my life has unfolded in ways I never consciously planned, yet somehow always pointed me here. I often think about what first drew me to this work, and what continues to give it meaning.

For me, it began long before I knew what marketing was. My father worked in what was then called promotions and sponsorship. Our garage was stacked floor to ceiling with boxes of branded merchandise: caps, pens, T-shirts, matchboxes. Each box was labelled neatly and carried the story of a brand he helped shape. I grew up surrounded by those colours and slogans, with brand identities as familiar as family. The smell of cardboard, the rustle of plastic wrapping and the satisfaction my father took in seeing a campaign come together was the soundtrack of my childhood.

I didn't realise it then, but I was growing up inside the architecture of storytelling. I saw how my father connected brands with causes, and how he found creative ways to align values and meaning long before 'purpose' became marketing jargon. For him, it was never just about transactions; it was about resonance, the feeling that something you built could connect people to an idea that mattered.

Even as a child, I began to sense that branding wasn't just about logos or products; it was about identity and emotion. Listening to my father's stories about the brands he managed, I learnt how each one carried a distinct personality—a voice, a character, a tone. I became fascinated by how certain brands attracted certain kinds of people. One brand could feel bold and masculine, while another could feel elegant, trustworthy and refined. That understanding became part of me, and it's one of the strengths I've carried into my own career; knowing how to read the energy of a brand, to understand who it speaks to and to align it with the people it serves.

Recently, when my father turned ninety, that connection came full circle. As we lit the candles on his birthday cake, someone opened a drawer and reached for a box of matches branded with a logo he once managed more than fifty years ago. The matches still worked. And while the brand no longer exists, everyone around the table recognised it immediately. It was a strange, moving reminder of how lasting ideas can be. Of how something created decades ago can outlive the business itself and still spark recognition, connection, even emotion. That small flame felt like legacy in its purest form.

Many of us carry invisible inheritances like that, not just in family, but in the environments that shaped us. For some, it's a parent's influence. For others, a defining hardship, a

WHY WE DO WHAT WE DO   **39**

teacher's encouragement or a moment that crystallised what truly mattered.

A friend of mine became a nurse after losing her brother in an accident. She remembers standing in the hospital corridor, surrounded by machines and urgency, feeling utterly helpless. Her brother was in intensive care, and despite the constant movement around her, she felt frozen—unable to do anything but watch. What haunted her most was the thought that in those final hours, he might have felt alone. That experience never left her. It became her reason for stepping into a career where she could make sure others would not have to face that kind of moment without care, without presence, without humanity.

Another friend built a career in sustainability after watching her grandparents' livelihood unravel on their small family farm. Year after year, the seasons became unpredictable. Droughts stretched longer, storms hit harder, and the harvests they'd once relied on with confidence grew uncertain. She saw the toll it took—not just on the land, but on their hope. The farm had been in their family for generations, but the weather no longer played by the old rules. That slow heartbreak planted a conviction in her that's never left: to dedicate her work to protecting what remains and helping others adapt before it's too late.

Our paths may look different, but the origin stories are often the same; experience leaves an imprint, and over time, that imprint becomes a compass.

We underestimate how early our relationship with work begins. It's learnt by observation; through the tone of dinner table conversations, the way adults talk about purpose or pressure, the stories they bring home at night. Some model work as a source of joy; others as a burden. Either way, those impressions take hold. They form our early definition of success long before we have words for it.

My father defined much of his life through his work. He was proud of what he built and how it made him feel: productive, useful, respected. When he retired, I watched him struggle to find that same sense of meaning. Like so many of his generation, his professional identity had been tightly woven into his self-worth, and the absence of work left a silence he didn't know how to fill. I learnt a lot from that season of his life. It taught me that while work can be a profound expression of who we are, it should never be the entirety of it. For me, marketing has become less about identity and more about expression. It's a creative outlet, a form of connection, a way of bringing ideas to life that move people or make a difference. That distinction matters. Identity confines; expression expands.

Over time, I've seen that our 'why' evolves with us. Early in our careers, it might be about proving ourselves. About mastery, progress or recognition. But as we grow, the motivation often shifts. We start to find more satisfaction in contribution, creativity and legacy. Sometimes we outgrow the ambitions that once fuelled us, but that's not loss—it's evolution. It's the natural expansion that comes from living and leading with awareness.

When we understand why we do what we do, it changes how we show up every day. It influences the tone we set, the patience we bring and the way we make decisions.

I think of a leader I worked with who began every team meeting by asking one simple question: 'Why does this matter?' It wasn't rhetorical; it anchored the conversation. It reminded everyone in the room that their work connected to something bigger than the task.

The people who lead with clarity of purpose don't need to chase momentum; they create it. They draw others in through conviction, not control. You can feel it in the way they show up—steady, intentional, grounded. These are the leaders whose calm presence cuts through chaos because their energy comes from alignment, not urgency.

I've noticed that when leaders lose touch with their original why, their work starts to flatten. Meetings become mechanical. Innovation fades. The spark that once animated their thinking turns into routine.

I remember a conversation with a creative director I deeply admired; someone who had built a remarkable career in advertising, led award-winning campaigns and mentored some of the brightest minds in the industry.

Over coffee one afternoon, he admitted that he no longer felt connected to the work. 'Everything runs smoothly,' he said, 'but I can't feel it anymore.' We started talking about what had first drawn him into the industry, and his face changed as he remembered. He spoke about being a teenager obsessed with storytelling, how he'd spent hours sketching ideas for commercials that made people laugh or cry and how, early in his career, he'd fallen in love with the power of an idea to make someone feel something.

But somewhere along the way, the rhythm had shifted. The deadlines multiplied. The meetings replaced the making. The metrics took centre stage. He realised that what had driven him wasn't the chase for awards or recognition, it was the magic of shaping ideas that moved people—and that this had been traded for efficiency. Reconnecting with that original 'why' transformed his leadership. He began carving out space in his calendar for creative sessions again, mentoring younger talent and pushing for ideas that didn't just meet objectives, but stirred emotion. The spark returned, and so did his team's belief in the work.

Reconnecting with our why doesn't just renew motivation, it reignites authenticity. It shapes how we treat people, how we hold space for others and how we navigate change. When we know what truly matters to us, we lead differently. We become steadier in our values, clearer in our choices and more compassionate towards those who are still finding their footing.

I often meet leaders who are restless or burnt out. They tell me they've lost their spark, that everything feels transactional. When I ask why they started doing this work in the first place, the answers are never about income or achievement. One founder told me she began her business after watching her mother struggle to access medical care in a rural town. Another executive remembered how a single teacher once believed in him when no one else did, and how that belief became the fuel behind his commitment to developing others.

Rediscovering those origin stories reconnects people with their humanity. It softens the edges. It reminds them that beneath every strategy, every goal and every quarterly review, there's something authentically human that once called them to do this work.

When we lead from that place—from our own sense of meaning and memory—we lead with more empathy and less ego. We listen differently. We notice more. We stop chasing validation and start building connection.

So I ask you to consider:

- What first called you to do what you do?

- Can you still feel that sense of meaning in your day-to-day, or has it become inaudible beneath the noise?

- When was the last time your work truly felt alive, and what made it so?

- And if you were to strip away the job title, the targets, the expectations, what remains that still feels true?

8

The Rational Case
for Creative Courage

IT'S EASY TO TALK about courage when you're not the one
signing off on the budget.

I've spent enough time in boardrooms and budget reviews
to know this: most creative courage isn't loud, and it's rarely
celebrated in the moment. More often, it looks like holding
your ground in a room full of doubt. Protecting an idea that
isn't fully formed. Backing your team when a safer path is on
the table. Choosing to wait or choosing to go first can both
be brave, depending on the context.

I've been thinking a lot about courage lately. Not the grand
kind that wins awards or makes headlines, but the modest,
rational kind that happens every day when you're leading
people and ideas. Whether you're managing a creative team,
launching a new product or pushing for change in a complex
system, that kind of courage matters.

We often think of creativity and courage as emotional con-
cepts. But I'd like to argue that they're also highly rational.

It's important to know this, especially now, when it feels like creative confidence is under pressure. Despite all the data that proves bold ideas drive better business outcomes, many companies still hesitate to take risks. Some see themselves as risk-friendly, but a large number—by their own admission—remain highly risk-averse.

Why does this matter? Because companies that embrace creative risk are more likely to see long-term growth. Research shows that bold brands are not only more distinctive, they often produce higher profit margins, stronger customer relationships and greater cultural relevance. So while playing it safe might feel smart in the short term, it often leads to the very outcomes leaders are trying to avoid—wasted spend, declining relevance, and uninspired teams who stop pushing for better.

Here's where I think the misunderstanding lies: creative courage is often equated with recklessness. But that's not what the best work is built on. The smartest creative risks I've seen, and helped bring to life, are rooted in two things: strong insights and strong teams.

I recall taking a creative approach to a new product I had to pitch in a very conservative boardroom. The initial reaction? Silence. The idea was unconventional. It didn't fit the category norms or the conservative approach of my predecessor, and there were easier, safer routes that could be taken. But the insight behind my approach was undeniable; it tapped into a fundamental human quality that competitors had overlooked. And one board member in that room calmly said exactly what I wanted to hear, 'Why don't we just try it?'

That small act of courage changed everything. The product launch and campaign went on to outperform every metric because the approach connected emotionally, as well as rationally. And what stayed with me wasn't just the results, it was that moment—of trust, of taking a chance—when belief outweighed fear.

Insights are the stabiliser. Without them, you're not being brave; you're guessing. But when you've done the work, and when the insight is real and sharp and culturally resonant, the risk becomes calculated. You know why you're making the move and what it's meant to do.

I've seen this in teams where mutual respect and shared ambition exist—in agencies, corporate settings and cross-functional teams. The strongest work is almost always born from a partnership in which both sides invest in each other, stay curious and chase something real.

It's not always easy, but it's worth it.

And yet, even when the insights are solid, many organisations struggle to act fast enough. Decision-making is delayed by red tape, layered approvals and the fear of getting it wrong. The result? Missed opportunities. Watered-down ideas. Innovation that stalls before it starts.

As a leader, I've felt this tension, too. We want bold work, but we also want certainty. We want standout ideas, but we want alignment. The paradox is real. But creative effectiveness requires us to streamline, not stall. To empower teams, not just protect outcomes.

One of the most useful things I've learnt is how to build 'fast tracks' inside a system. To know when something needs ten stakeholders and when it only needs two. And to be clear with teams about where they have space to move, and where they need to come back. But it's not just about speed. It's also about trust, and trust, I've found, is the greatest accelerator of all.

I recently heard a strategist remind a whole roomful of people that clients are people too. They're navigating uncertainty and expectation, and under pressure to deliver results. It reminded me that leadership is about protecting both ideas and people. It's about making the space where creativity can happen. Holding the line when everyone else wants to dilute. Knowing when to say, 'Let's go,' and when to say, 'Not yet.'

When I think about the bold decisions that stuck—campaigns and product launches, yes, but also team initiatives and leadership calls that changed the tone or moved the needle—I realise that every one of them required someone to go first. That someone had to be vulnerable in the pitch. They had to back an unconventional route and fight for the insight. They had to stay curious, even when the data wasn't neat.

That's creative courage. Not bravado. Not chaos. Just brave clarity.

Recently, a creative leader told me that their team had stopped presenting bold ideas because, over time, the feedback had become too sharp. Too practical. Too focused on what couldn't be done. It made me wonder: are we unknowingly training our teams to shrink? Are we, as leaders, prioritising polish over possibility? Certainty over stretch? And more importantly, how do we make it safe again—not to play it safe, but safe enough to try something brave?

Creative courage isn't limited to marketing. It's what lets a founder take a new path, a teacher try a new method or a leader back an idea before it's proven. In any field, it's what keeps progress alive.

So I invite you to consider:

- Where are you playing it too safe in the name of being responsible?

- What might change if you reframed creative courage as a rational, strategic act that protects progress, not just process?

- When was the last time belief outweighed your fear, even briefly?

- And how might you lead in a way that says to your team, 'It's okay to go there. I've got you.'

9

Visibility vs. Impact

NOT ALL LEADERSHIP is visible. And not all visibility is leadership.

That truth has been with me for a while. It appears in moments when the applause goes to the loudest voice or the most polished presentation, even if someone else was doing the quiet lifting behind the scenes. It appears in team meetings where the same few people speak up, while others do the foundational work that holds the entire effort together. And it shows up in the mirror, too. Especially in seasons when you're giving your all, but the spotlight lands elsewhere.

I've lived both sides of this. There have been times I've been in the spotlight: keynote speaker, campaign lead, spokesperson. And there have been times I've done the invisible work: helping a teammate get unstuck, rewriting slides at midnight, silently stitching together a fractured project. One garners recognition. The other builds the muscle of leadership.

Visibility can be rewarding. But it can also be deceptive.

It's easy to mistake visibility for value. And in a metrics-driven world, that confusion can be reinforced by likes, headlines and dashboards. But the impact we create is often unseen. Impact is the late-night coaching call. The extra pass that lets someone else shine. The decision to step back so someone else can step up. Leadership is measured in outcomes, but it's revealed in those moments when no one is watching.

Years ago, one of my team members was nominated for a company award. They didn't know it at the time, but I had advocated fiercely for them behind the scenes. They had done extraordinary work, not just in delivery, but in culture, mentorship and resilience. But they weren't someone who self-promoted. They didn't seek the spotlight. In many ways, they were underestimated.

Their reaction when they won? Humble disbelief. It reminded me that sometimes the most meaningful leadership act isn't to be seen—it's making sure others are.

Of course, visibility has its place. We need visible role models. We need people who speak up, show up and hold the line when it counts. But it's just one part of the picture. It can't be the only currency. This tension often arises in high-performance environments. There's pressure to show value and to prove you belong. And it can make you feel like if you're not in the room, you don't matter. If your work isn't praised publicly, it wasn't meaningful. If you didn't get credit, you didn't contribute.

But real leadership isn't always post-able.

It looks like leaning in on a weekend to support a struggling team. It sounds like redirecting credit when someone else deserves it. It feels like holding space in hard conversations, even when it costs you political capital. And sometimes, it simply means knowing the difference between being important and being useful.

I once worked with a senior leader who quietly mentored three future directors across departments, none of whom reported to him. Years later, when those leaders rose through the ranks, each of them credited him privately for their confidence and clarity. His name was never mentioned in the announcements, but his fingerprints were everywhere.

In my own journey, I've learnt when to step forward and when to step back. I've had to unlearn the reflex to perform for recognition and replace it with a deeper intention: to lead with purpose. I don't always get it right. But I try to stay anchored in a question that has become a personal compass: Am I showing up for impact, or for attention? If the answer is attention, I pause. If it's impact, I proceed.

There have been times when that balance felt like walking a tightrope. I've had moments when stepping forward was the right thing to do, and I used my seniority or position to make sure an idea was heard, or to help someone on my team get the recognition they deserved. But leadership visibility can be a tricky currency. In the effort to move things forward, sometimes the attention has landed back on me, even when that wasn't the intention. It's uncomfortable; you want progress, not spotlight. But those moments have taught me that influence isn't about avoiding visibility, it's about directing it; using it with intention, then stepping aside so others can own the space they've earned.

In the long game of leadership, it's the impact that compounds. It's what people remember when the campaigns have ended and the titles have changed. It isn't about how brightly you're seen, but how deeply you make things better for others.

So I invite you to consider:

- Where are you making a difference, even if no one sees it?

- What does impact look like for you, beyond recognition and reward?

- And how might you honour the quiet forms of leadership, in both yourself and in others—the ones that don't trend, but truly transform?

10

Final Call: The Courage to Choose

THERE'S A MOMENT in every journey when the gate is about to close. The final boarding call is made, late passengers are called over the PA system, and there's a brief window, just seconds long, where a choice must be made: to move forward or to stay.

Some of us have experienced that sprint through the terminal. That pause at the café, wondering if you really have time for a coffee. That glance back at the screen before committing. You move, or you don't. And once the door is shut, it's shut.

Leadership is filled with moments like these. Not as dramatic or time-stamped, but just as decisive.

We don't always know we're facing a final call. Sometimes it feels like a routine decision. Other times it's wrapped in uncertainty, without a blinking deadline to force our hand.

But we often sense it somewhere deep down; the weight of the moment, the shift it signals. And still, we hesitate.

Why? Because the final choice means leaving something behind. A version of safety. A familiar rhythm. An identity we've outgrown but haven't fully released. The final call isn't just about what you're stepping into, it's about what you're leaving behind.

The challenge isn't in the logistics. It's in the emotional readiness, and that readiness rarely shows up on time.

So we delay. We seek more data. We ask one more opinion. We tweak the plan again. We wait for the perfect moment. But clarity doesn't always come before the call. Often, it comes after. After we move and commit. After we trust our instincts more than the spreadsheet.

I remember once turning down a job offer that everyone assumed I'd take. On paper, it seemed perfect: the title, the package, the promise. But something in me knew it wasn't right: the culture, the pace, the cost. Saying no felt uncomfortable at the time—almost counterintuitive. Months later, that company restructured, and I realised I had chosen alignment over ambition without even realising it. Sometimes the reward for listening to yourself isn't applause, it's peace.

In leadership, final calls aren't just career shifts or structural changes. They're decisions about how we want to show up, who we're becoming and what we're no longer willing to tolerate. They're the invisible turning points that can ultimately define our direction. You might not realise it was a final call until later, until the team dynamic changes. Until the trust deepens. Until you feel lighter, clearer, more whole. Or, perhaps for a while, more alone. Because every choice has a cost.

And, of course, not all final calls feel good in the moment. Some come with grief, uncertainty and temporary silence where applause used to be. But in that silence, something else becomes audible—the deeper knowing that you've chosen alignment over approval. Courage over comfort. Growth over familiarity.

I once watched a leader choose to end a long-running initiative her team had poured months of effort into because the strategy no longer made sense. She faced resistance and disappointment, but much later, that single act of honesty became the foundation for one of the most loyal teams I've ever seen. Integrity doesn't always look like progress; sometimes it looks like pause.

These choices may not announce themselves. Sometimes they look like backing out of a panel you said yes to but know doesn't serve your energy. Sometimes they look like standing firm in a room where consensus is easier. Sometimes they look like leaving a role, a company or a project when nothing is visibly wrong—except that it's no longer right.

And other times, the choice is to stay. To recommit and deepen your roots instead of seeking new ground. Staying can be just as courageous as leaving if it's conscious and aligned. If it's not driven by fear, but by clarity.

What matters is that you hear the call. That you don't silence it with noise or delay. That you pause long enough to ask: Is this a pivotal moment? And if so, what does it require of me?

It's okay if the answer doesn't come in a rush. Sometimes, it arrives like a whisper. A recurring thought. A bodily cue. A creative pull that won't go away. A moment of discomfort that reveals something deeper. That's what clarity often looks like in leadership—not a neon sign, but a steady insistence. When you tune in, you may realise the choice has been there, waiting for you, for a long time. And that once made, that choice will reshape more than just your calendar. It will reshape how you lead and listen and spend your time. How others respond to your energy. Because when a leader is in alignment, even if the road ahead is unclear, there's a steadiness that others can feel.

You won't always get it right. Some choices might need course correction. But the act of choosing and owning the call is where your power resides.

We live in a world of infinite options. That reality makes the art of decision-making more critical than ever.

The path ahead is no longer linear. Many leaders are building portfolio careers, and juggling board seats, advisory roles and creative pursuits alongside their day jobs. The rise of fractional executives has redefined what commitment looks like.

For younger generations, the idea of a single, lifelong employer feels foreign. They want flexibility, impact and autonomy in equal measure.

In this landscape, clarity is your compass. The challenge isn't the lack of opportunity, it's the abundance of it. Every 'yes' reshapes what remains possible, and every 'no' is a declaration of what matters most.

I've seen this play out in coaching conversations. A brilliant strategist turned down a global role to stay anchored in a community project that gave her a sense of purpose she couldn't find in a title. Another friend left corporate life entirely to work part-time across two start-ups, describing her choice as 'trading stability for sovereignty.' Their choices looked unconventional, but both found something that felt true: alignment between their work and the lives they wanted to lead.

This is the new art of leadership; not just choosing between roles, but conducting the rhythm of your career. The courage to define success on your own terms is, itself, a final call.

And with so many paths available, discernment becomes its own form of leadership. We cannot lead everything. We cannot say yes to every opportunity, every request, every version of ourselves. There comes a moment when we have to choose what we're not becoming, so that we can fully become what we are.

Final calls help us do that. They draw a line. They create focus. They sharpen the work, the words and the energy. They make us braver. But only if we hear them. And only if we're willing to respond, not react.

So I invite you to consider:

- What choice has been waiting for you?
- Where are you standing at the gate, holding a ticket, but hesitating to board?
- What are you afraid to leave behind and what might open up if you did?

11

Grace in
the Grey

AMBIGUITY AND COMPLEXITY are often mentioned in the same breath. But they're not the same thing.

Ambiguity is the absence of clarity, and in leadership, and in today's leadership environments, it's a constant that we're expected to navigate. Complexity, on the other hand, is the presence of multiple, sometimes conflicting truths that must be held at once. Ambiguity is not knowing what to do; complexity is knowing exactly what must be done and still finding it hard.

And that's the grey—the space where something can be right and still hurt. Where head and heart, progress and people, conviction and care all collide.

The ability to lead through that tension, to hold two truths at once, is one of the most human leadership skills I've learnt. It's the tension of doing what's best for the business while knowing it will hurt some of the people who helped build it. It might mean making the call to restructure, even when you carry the weight of what it means for individuals. Or celebrating a new direction, while privately grieving what it cost to get there.

These are not hypotheticals. This is the reality many leaders are experiencing right now: global layoffs, paused initiatives, decisions made for the long term that carry short-term pain. Moments when what's necessary and what's human are in tension. When your values are clear, but your path isn't.

And the fact is, the grey has become almost constant. Many people today are leading, or simply working, through seasons of acute uncertainty: economic pressures, evolving industries and teams stretched thin after repeated cycles of change. It's not just leaders who feel the weight, it's everyone trying to do good work while wondering if stability means anything anymore.

A fellow CMO told me she feels like she's leading in a permanent state of triage—steadying one team while another is hit by change. Her reflection stayed with me: 'It's not the change itself that's hard, it's the pace that never stops.'

The air of vulnerability that engulfs many workplaces today is part of the new reality of leadership.

There's a natural impulse in leadership to resolve, explain and tie things up with clarity. We want to be reassuring, decisive, certain. But the grey doesn't always need to be fixed. Sometimes it needs to be held—with honesty, with integrity and with grace.

And that kind of leadership takes practice.

It takes courage to stand in the in-between, where your decisions don't please everyone but you know they're necessary. It takes empathy to sit beside someone's disappointment, even when you can't offer a different outcome. It takes self-awareness to acknowledge that even the right decision can carry a cost: emotionally, relationally or reputationally.

It also takes stamina. Because the grey can last longer than expected. It's not always a moment; sometimes it's a season. And when there's no clear endpoint, grace becomes essential—not as softness or avoidance, but as presence and humanity. It's the ability to acknowledge the full emotional landscape while still moving forward with care.

There are moments after tough decisions, even the ones you know are right, when silence lingers. There's a loneliness that can follow those moments. I remember one vividly—it was a call that affected a small but beloved part of a team. The silence after the announcement was heavy. I went home that night and couldn't shake it. That's when I realised leadership can mean holding space for outcomes your heart doesn't celebrate, even when your head knows they're right.

And that ability to hold both conviction and compassion— to stay open-hearted even when the outcome hurts—is what makes leadership honest.

Grace also shows up in smaller moments. When a team member is struggling and you know the project needs to move faster, but you choose to slow down and support them anyway. When someone brings you difficult feedback and, instead of defending, you thank them. When you're proud of your team's achievements, but also aware of the fatigue they don't always voice. It shows up when you're juggling stakeholder priorities and choose to advocate for the long-term idea that doesn't have easy metrics. Or when you acknowledge that something could have been done better, even if no one else saw the cracks. And sometimes, it looks like saying, 'I don't have the answer yet,' and being okay with the discomfort that follows. Leaders are expected to bring certainty, but grace allows us to bring honesty.

These are the invisible layers of leadership that rarely make it onto KPIs or dashboards. The decisions no one sees. The nuance you hold behind the scenes. The grace in the grey.

You won't always get it right. You'll misread a situation, you'll say yes when you should have said no, you'll try to protect someone and it won't be enough. That's part of it. What matters is not perfection, but how you choose to respond.

Grace, in those moments, is returning to what grounds you. Recommitting to lead with the kind of intention you'd want from someone leading you.

And sometimes, it's about forgiving yourself—for being human, for carrying the weight, for not having the perfect words in the moment. That, too, is part of grace. And that's why grace matters, because the grey doesn't end—it just changes form.

I remember a time when every week seemed to bring another hard call. A restructure. A strategy pivot. A difficult conversation that couldn't wait. I would hold it together all day—calm, composed, steady—then drive home in silence and feel the weight of what it meant for the people involved. It wasn't regret, exactly, but the heaviness of knowing that right and hard can live in the same decision.

To me, a real test of leadership isn't how quickly you resolve the hard things, but how human you can remain while carrying them. Because this is where real leadership dwells; not in the extremes, but in the stretch. Not in certainty, but in how we hold complexity with care.

So I invite you to consider:

- Where in your life or leadership are you standing in the grey right now?

- What does grace look like in that space?

- And how might you stay grounded in compassion, even when clarity feels out of reach?

Belief as a Leadership Practice

NE OF the most powerful things you can offer someone as a leader is your belief. Not just in their output, but in their potential; in how they think, what
they might become, and how they handle the stretch before
they feel ready. Belief, when given early, has a compounding
effect and can create the moment that rewires how someone
sees themself.

I've always seen belief as part of my job. When I spot talent—
real, raw or still forming—I say it out loud. I tell them: 'I have
complete faith in you.' Or 'I have no doubt you can deliver.'

Because those words matter. They land. They stay with
people. And more often than not, they become the reason
someone takes the leap into a bigger role, a braver idea, or
a room they weren't planning to step into yet.

I remember when I said those words to a young woman on my team who'd just stepped into her first major leadership project. She was brilliant but hesitant, convinced she wasn't ready. I told her plainly, 'You've got this—I wouldn't have given you the brief if I didn't trust you completely.' And she did 'get it'. Not perfectly, but her confidence grew each week. Watching her self-belief catch up to my belief in her reminded me how powerful those moments can be—when someone sees in themselves what you've seen all along.

That's what belief does. It doesn't just offer encouragement, it creates momentum.

I've seen people stand taller simply because someone trusted them out loud. I've seen good talent become great simply because they were given room to grow and reminded, often, that they belonged there.

That's not about performance reviews or promotion cycles. It's about presence. Consistent, intentional belief that's present in the everyday moments: the one-on-one, the project kick-off, the murmured, 'You've got this,' when the pressure hits.

A peer once told me his best boss never flinched in a crisis. Instead, she'd simply say, 'I trust your judgement—go.' That kind of permission, he said, changed how he led his own team years later.

Belief is not a soft skill. It's a leadership discipline. And in my experience, it's one of the most transformative. It's easy to assume people know they're doing well, that they must feel confident if they're performing. But belief and confidence don't always travel together. Some of the most capable peo-ple I've worked with have been the slowest to see their own growth. Especially those who lead with humility. Or are new to the room. Or who haven't yet seen a version of themselves in leadership. In these situations, belief becomes a bridge between uncertainty and action, between hesitation and momentum. It transforms someone quietly doing the work into someone ready to lead it.

And it's not just about the big statements. Sometimes belief is expressed in the way you give someone space without micromanaging. Or in how you listen—really listen—to their ideas in a meeting. Or in how you pause after they speak, instead of rushing in to clarify. People notice those things. Especially early in their journey. And especially when they're used to being overlooked.

Of course, belief has to be real. It's not about inflating egos or glossing over growth areas. It's about spotting potential and naming it. About offering trust early, so someone can build into it. And about holding space for someone to grow, without needing them to prove they're already there.

I've had the privilege of seeing what happens when people receive that kind of belief and choose to carry it forward. They start offering it to others. They start leading with a lighter touch and a longer view. They become generous with their energy and anchored in something bigger than performance. That's how belief spreads. That's how it becomes culture.

I think we often underestimate how hungry people are to be believed in. Especially in fast-paced environments, where feedback loops are short and success is measured in slides, metrics and delivery. But belief isn't about waiting for someone to tick every box. It's about saying, 'I see it in you already.' And meaning it.

That doesn't mean we stop challenging people. In fact, it's the opposite. When someone knows you believe in them, they're more likely to stretch, to speak up, to stay the course when things get hard. Belief gives people resilience. And resilience creates leaders.

I keep coming back to this: belief isn't something you reserve for the standout moments. It's something you practise, in the small ways, every day. Say the words. Offer the trust. Cast the vote. Because you never know what someone will become when they hear, maybe for the first time, that someone else believes they can.

So I invite you to consider:

- Who in your world could use your belief right now, even if they haven't asked for it?

- How might your leadership change if belief became a daily discipline rather than an occasional gesture?

- And what could shift in your culture if everyone led with that same intent?

13

Performing Under Pressure

EADERSHIP ISN'T JUST about vision or values. It's also about delivery. The pressure to perform is a real and constant presence, and the higher you go, the sharper that pressure can feel.

Revenue. Growth. Market share. These aren't abstract ideals. They're expectations tied to boardroom conversations and market dynamics. And delivering on them is part of the job. But performance under pressure is rarely clean. And I've learnt, sometimes the hard way, that staying focused on results without losing clarity, style or sanity takes more than discipline. It takes pause and perspective.

Because urgency is loud. It fills calendars. It fuels adrenaline. And when you're in a high-growth environment, it can start to feel like speed equals success. I've seen many leaders fall into that trap. Racing to respond, pushing to deliver, and forgetting to ask if we're moving in the right direction—or just moving fast.

I've fallen into that trap. Caught myself measuring progress by how many meetings I'd made it through, not by what had actually moved forward. It took an exhausted Friday night flight home to realise I'd been mistaking activity for impact.

Leading through pressure starts with discernment. What matters most right now? What directly shifts the outcome? What can wait? And what, if I'm honest, no longer serves us? The best leaders I know treat focus like currency; they spend it where it counts and protect it fiercely.

Sometimes it's not about doing more, but choosing better. I try to come back to that idea often. And when I do, things start to clear. Because performance isn't a solo sport. The best results I've seen in my career have come from teams who feel connected to the goal and, importantly, each other. That connection doesn't come from reporting lines or KPIs. It comes from belief. Belief in the work. Belief in the team. Belief that what we're doing matters, and that we have what it takes to do it well.

One of the most high-performing teams I ever led wasn't the one with the biggest budget, but the one that had built genuine trust. They challenged ideas, shared ownership, and reminded each other of the 'why' when things got hard. That belief became our buffer against burnout.

Especially when pressure is high, I've learnt to create space to uncover what's going on beneath the surface. To know not just how we're tracking, but what's slowing things down, what's unclear, or what's taking more energy than it should.

I don't always ask this directly, but I try to notice the signs: a covert look across the table, a hesitant 'we're fine' that means we're not. Those moments are leadership cues—so pay attention. This practice has helped me remember that my job isn't just to hold the goal, it's to help others get there with clarity and care, and by using whatever rhythm they need to get the right outcome.

For me, this is less about rigid routines and more about respecting the different rhythms of each team member's life. We all work differently, and we all carry different loads: at home, at work and in between. So I try to find ways to help those rhythms co-exist and complement one another, not compete. That might mean anchoring the team around a few clear priorities each week, or creating space to align on what must be delivered; not everything, but the things that truly matter. When that alignment happens, the team breathes a little easier. Momentum builds, and we start to move together not just at pace, but with purpose.

In fast-moving environments, recognition also matters, for effort as well as outcomes. I try to notice the thinking behind a great presentation, the care shown in a customer moment or the grace someone shows under pressure. Because performance isn't only about output; it's also about the intent behind it. And acknowledging that effort fuels belief, especially when people are running hard.

Another lesson I've learnt over the years is the value of creating space. In high-pressure seasons, our default is to fill. Fill the calendar. Fill the pipeline. Fill the deck. But space is what lets people focus. And focus is what drives performance. Sometimes that means removing a report that adds no value. Or protecting a colleague's time when they need to go deep on something strategic. Or backing a teammate when they say no to a request that would dilute their impact. These are small things, but they're not soft. They're leadership in action. Do I always get this right? No. Sometimes we're moving so fast that even the thought of making space feels out of reach. But when I do create the time, I see the difference. And so does my team.

Clarity helps here, too. When the pressure spikes, and it will, clarity becomes your compass. It helps you lead from calm, not chaos. And that changes how people feel and how they show up.

It's in the in-between that I reconnect with this. That I remind myself performance isn't just the result, it's the tone we set in the way we deliver it. It's the question we ask before the meeting starts. The moment we choose not to escalate. The decision to prioritise progress over perfection. Performance is shaped in these moments, not just measured in the final ones. Because yes, the metrics matter. But the mindset behind them? That's what sustains performance. That's what helps a team feel proud, not just productive. And that's what builds a leadership style that lasts longer than any number.

So I invite you to consider:

- How are you supporting your team's ability to deliver under pressure?

- Are you reinforcing clarity, or reacting to urgency?

- What would it look like to protect space, not just fill it?

- And how might you lead from calm, so your team can perform from strength?

14

Creativity, Risk and Everything In Between

CREATIVITY, INTEGRITY and risk often travel together. Not always in the spotlight, but often in the wings. In the quiet decisions, the long meetings, the choices that leave a mark, even if no one sees them.

These ideas tend to get siloed. Creativity is for the artists. Integrity is for ethics. Risk is for entrepreneurs. But in practice, especially in leadership, they rarely travel alone. They twist together; challenging, testing and ultimately strengthening each other. Their tension, their interplay, often lives just beneath our most meaningful decisions. This is the kind of creativity that shapes direction. That reimagines what's possible. That leads with intention, even when there is no roadmap.

Creativity invites us to see the world differently. It asks us to imagine new paths, to reframe problems, to say something original—not just louder or faster. And while we celebrate creativity in its final form—the polished idea, the bold campaign, the breakthrough moment—its real value is seeded long before anything is visible.

Creative leadership isn't about chasing boldness for the sake of it. It's about having the courage to stay close to what matters and to shape ideas with care, not ego. To honour the voice inside that says, 'This feels right,' even when the world prefers something more polished. And that's where integrity begins to anchor us. Creative integrity is about staying true to the essence of an idea. It's the silent discipline of honouring what matters, even when there's pressure to smooth the edges, move faster or make something more acceptable.

My career has gifted me the privilege of guiding incredible brands through bold creative leaps. And looking back, the most meaningful work—the kind that still makes me proud—wasn't just about the end product. It was about trust. Trust in my instincts. Trust in my agency partners, who truly understood the brief behind the brief. And trust in the power of creative courage, even when the metrics weren't guaranteed.

But this kind of bravery doesn't just belong in campaign briefs. It's there in how we lead. In how we listen. In the decisions we make when no one is watching. When we protect an idea that hasn't quite found its voice. When we choose the harder conversation because it's the right one. When we pause long enough to ask: Is this truly what we believe? Because creative leadership isn't just about having brave ideas; it's about holding them with care, shaping them with intention and standing by them even when it's hard to explain.

I remember a leadership meeting years ago. In a boardroom walled with glass on the top floor of the building, above a city bleeding orange at 6:30 p.m., I watched a great idea slowly bend to accommodate every stakeholder voice. A line changed here, a frame softened there. No one meant harm—just consensus. By the time the room emptied, the idea was intact on paper and shattered in spirit. The buzz that comes from believing in something bold had slipped out with the catering trolley.

Integrity isn't about being inflexible. But it is about knowing when to hold your ground. It lives in the small choices. Do I speak up when I know something's off? Do I stand by a principle when popularity would be easier? Do I stay in alignment with what I believe, even when the pace or pressure tries to pull me out of it?

It's easy to mistake compromise for collaboration; to believe that accommodating something to get a peaceful outcome, bending something 'just for now,' won't matter. Because over time, those tiny turns accumulate. And the more often we honour what we know to be true, the stronger our self-trust becomes. That's the foundation of creative integrity.

And then comes risk.

It's tempting to associate risk with recklessness—big leaps, bold bets and loud decisions. But most of the risk we choose to take in leadership is more subtle. It looks like saying yes to an idea that doesn't yet have the numbers. Or trusting your gut when others are waiting for certainty. Or choosing the less obvious path because it feels right. It's not always quitting a job or launching something new. Sometimes it's speaking up when silence would be easier. Sometimes it's choosing to wait.

Calculated risk isn't about being fearless. It's about being awake to the cost of staying still. There's risk in change, but also in inertia. There's risk in speaking up, but also in silence. There's risk in backing something new, but also in clinging to what no longer serves.

Taking risk with integrity means anchoring to purpose, not performance. It's asking: What am I really trying to protect? And am I being led by clarity or by fear?

I once heard a fellow CMO describe a late-night 'war room' session during a global campaign review –11:45 p.m., fluorescent lights humming, walls covered in Post-its, pizza boxes on the table. The 'safe' route was taking the metric-driven approach and sailing through approvals. Instead, they pulled call-centre transcripts onto the table, found a sharper insight, piloted the braver idea in one region, and only then scaled. More risk, yes—but anchored in integrity and insight. It reminded me that creative risk doesn't have to be reckless. It just has to be real.

Some of the most defining moments of my career, and my life, didn't come with a playbook. They came with a small but persistent knowing: a gut feeling that I knew the right decision or way forward. They asked me to back an idea before others could see it. To speak a truth that wasn't yet popular. To trust that making the right choice was more important than applause.

And this tension isn't just professional. We carry it into how we lead, how we parent, how we rest, and how we relate to ourselves and others.

When my son was younger, he loved Transformers and, thankfully, each one came with a detailed instruction manual—or else they'd be almost impossible to assemble! One day, after a parenting decision he didn't fully understand, I said to him, 'You get a manual with your Transformers. But Mum didn't get one of those to be your mum. I just have to do what I feel is best for you.' He laughed, and it became something of a shared line between us. It was a gentle reminder that not everything comes with clear steps, and that even in the absence of certainty, we lead anyway.

That's what creativity with integrity looks like: leading with care, trusting your instincts, and standing by your choices even when they don't come with guarantees.

I remember a regional strategy session in which a business challenge had already been solved on paper. The recommendation was sound, data-backed and safe. The room was quiet, everyone nodding along. But was this a missed opportunity? I decided to ask a simple question: 'If we were to start from scratch, what would we do differently?'

I wasn't trying to challenge the proposed solution, just widen the view. Rather than diving deeper into data points or implementation timelines, the conversation shifted towards what could be possible if we approached the problem differently. It reignited belief that we could achieve more not by spending more, but by thinking more creatively about how to get there. That moment reminded me that creativity in leadership is about unlocking better outcomes by asking better questions and holding space for possibility—even when the path ahead isn't clear. Because that's where creativity, risk and integrity often meet; in the space between what is and what could be.

So I invite you to consider:

- Where in your world are creativity, integrity and risk intersecting?

- Is there a decision, idea or conversation that could benefit from being seen through a more creative lens?

- What question could you ask that might open a new path forward?

- And how might you hold that space with clarity, courage and care—long enough to see what could emerge in between?

15

Legacy
Without Ego

IN LEADERSHIP, LEGACY is often wrapped in the language of achievement: titles held, milestones reached, empires built. But I've never been wired that way. I've never chased the next promotion or aimed for the most prestigious job title in the room. For me, legacy has always been more personal.

What if it's not about the footprint you leave behind, but about the space you made while you were here? Not about how loud your impact echoed, but how deeply it endured? Legacy lives in two places: in people and in the work itself. It's the culture you build and the progress that continues after you've gone.

Ego plays a central role in how we think about influence; the need to be seen, the desire to be known for something, the temptation to leave a mark so clear that it cannot be erased. But influence built on ego fades. The kind that lasts comes from intention and purpose, and from creating work and environments that can survive without you.

Real legacy, the kind I want to leave, isn't ego-led. It's purpose-led. It shows up in both people and progress. It's there in the conversations no one else hears, in the encouragement that sparks self-belief in another, in the systems you build and the brands that grow because you gave them a strong foundation. It's in work that keeps working, even when your name is no longer attached.

I've always wanted to be known as a remarkable leader—not for being the loudest voice, but for being the kind of leader people feel safe with, stretched by and seen by. I want the people I've worked with to look back and think, 'That was a time I grew.'

Leadership without ego doesn't mean shrinking or stepping back. It means showing up with presence and purpose, but without needing to be the centre of the story. It's building something that doesn't fall apart when you step away. And it's mentoring others to rise knowing their success might eclipse your own, and being at peace with that.

Some of the proudest moments in my career haven't come from the roles I've held, but from the people I've had the privilege of leading. I've seen them fill bigger roles: some have stepped into C-suite positions, others have led large teams or major brands. They didn't always see their own potential at first, but something in them sparked when given space, encouragement and belief.

I think often about one of my former assistants, who started in an administrative role but was curious about marketing. One day, I asked her what she was most interested in learning. Her eyes lit up as she spoke about a particular area of marketing, so we made a plan. I gave her opportunities to shadow projects and take on small tasks in that discipline, and helped train her to build confidence. Over time, she grew; first in skill, then in voice, then in leadership. Gradually, she took on more and more responsibility for that portfolio. Today, she's the national brand manager for the very discipline she expressed an interest in. Watching her rise has been one of my proudest professional accomplishments. Not because of what I taught her, but because I helped open the door early enough for her to walk through it on her own. Her success reaffirmed that, when given early, belief can change the course of someone's career. To help create the conditions for others to thrive is the kind of legacy I treasure most.

There's a strength in leading this way. A leader who operates without ego doesn't need to own every idea. They're not shaken by disagreement. They don't need the credit. They see succession as a responsibility, not a threat. They understand that success multiplies when it's shared.

This kind of leadership has been most tested for me in times of crisis. There have been moments when the path ahead wasn't clear and the stakes were high, and I've had to rely on intuition more than instruction. In these moments I've had to listen intently, lead with care and give people priority over process. I wasn't always sure of the answer, but I knew what mattered most—not just looking after people's roles, but looking after their lives.

I saw this modelled by a regional CEO during a period of grave uncertainty. As the business faced restructuring, she gathered her team—not to announce decisions, but to ask, 'What do you need from me to keep going?' That question shifted the energy instantly. It reminded everyone that strength in leadership is measured not by control, but by composure and care, and that the most lasting legacies are built on how people felt in the hardest moments.

It's not easy to lead this way. Especially in industries where personal brand and public recognition are currency. In meetings where the loudest voice often wins. In organisations where climbing is mistaken for leading. But ego doesn't build trust. And ego doesn't build teams.

Choosing humility in those rooms isn't soft, it's strategic. And it's what gives people room to grow. There's something beautiful about the leaders who build without needing to be in the frame. They don't need the spotlight because they've helped shine it on others. They speak last to let others be heard. They're not absent, they're profoundly present. And their presence is the reason others feel brave enough to step up.

Their teams thrive—not in spite of them, but because of them. Psychological safety grows. Accountability becomes shared. Creativity flows; not because the team is fearless, but because they're not afraid to be real. These leaders create space for contribution, for experimentation, for learning. And for leadership to grow beyond themselves.

Legacy without ego isn't about doing less, it's about choosing differently. It's saying yes to the work that matters, not just the work that's seen. It's investing in people even when that effort is invisible to the boardroom. It's making decisions that serve the next generation, not just the next quarter.

Legacy also abides in the work itself. I once led the first meeting with the CEO of a major telecommunications company to begin a complete rebrand of the organisation. We determined a direction that would see the company embark on over three years of work to get to the outcome agreed on in that very session.

Even after leaving an organisation, there's immense satisfaction in seeing the path you helped shape continue, knowing your creative fingerprints became part of a brand's enduring DNA.

Some of the most meaningful legacies don't bear names. They live in culture and in how people treat one another. Legacy can be found in the words 'This is just how we do things here.' What those words really mean is: we do things with integrity, with clarity, with care.

This kind of leadership also gives something back to the leader.

Ego asks us to prove ourselves over and over. Legacy without ego lets us breathe. It allows for rest. For delegation. For developing others, not just ourselves. It invites a broader version of success—one that is more sustainable and has a little more soul. There's courage in that too.

Letting go of ego means letting go of the belief that everything has to start with you and end with you. It means building systems that run without you and teams that flourish in your absence. It means trusting the people around you, and trusting that you've done the work to let them lead.

It also takes vision. Because legacy without ego isn't passive. It's intentional. It's not about being invisible. It's about knowing where your presence matters, and where your absence might empower even more. What lasts isn't the title. It's the way someone felt under your leadership. It's the bold idea that was backed because you made space for it. It's the quiet confidence that lingers long after the meeting ends. It's the team that still carries your values, even when they're charting their own path.

Legacy without ego is about being remembered for what you helped unlock. For who you saw. For the way you led when no one was watching. For how you showed up, and what you made possible.

So I invite you to consider:

- What are you building that doesn't need your name to last?

- Where are you leading with presence instead of prominence?

- What kind of legacy are you shaping—one that depends on you, or one that continues because of you?

- How might you lead today in a way that lasts—in people, in brands and in business—long after you've moved on?

16

Permission to Pause

SOMEWHERE ALONG THE WAY, we started equating pausing with falling behind.

We celebrate urgency, momentum and productivity. But presence? Stillness? That's harder to justify in a world that measures value by constant motion. And yet, I've learnt that the pause, even a brief one, can hold the clarity we're racing towards.

I spent years sprinting through packed calendars and long to-do lists, convinced that if I just got through the next week, month, quarter, it would all settle. But life doesn't hand out white space; it doesn't whisper, 'Now is a good time to rest.' We have to choose it, claim it and protect it.

And when we do, we remember something important—we are not machines. We are humans. And humans are not built for nonstop performance—we are meant to recharge, reflect and reorient before continuing. This isn't about dramatic sabbaticals or disappearing for weeks. Sometimes, the most powerful pause is a five-minute walk, a weekend without notifications, ten quiet minutes with a coffee before the day begins, or a question left unanswered for just one more day while you take a breath and think. Not because you're avoiding the answer, but because you're honouring the space where you will hear it.

For leaders, giving ourselves permission to pause can feel almost rebellious. It goes against everything we've been taught about showing up, being visible and pushing through. We've been conditioned to always be ready with an answer, a plan or a response. But when we allow even a little stillness into the mix, something subtle but powerful begins to happen. Urgency softens. Intuition surfaces. Our nervous systems relax and, often, so do our teams.

I used to think pausing was selfish or indulgent. But now I understand it as a leadership discipline that's a way of tuning in before tuning out. It's a moment to recalibrate, not retreat. Because when we run on empty, we don't lead well. We react. We grasp for quick wins, short-term fixes and certainty at any cost. We start to miss the nuance, the potential and the better question we didn't ask.

When we slow down, even briefly, we start to see things differently. We hear what's underneath the noise and notice what matters again. There's a reason clarity is often found in the shower, on a walk or during a long drive. It's not because we're trying harder, it's because we've finally stopped trying for just long enough to listen.

And that listening? That's where the real work begins.

Pausing doesn't mean you're giving up. It means you're checking in with yourself and the direction you're heading in— as well as the impact you're having and want to have. It's where courage and clarity meet. Not in the sprint, but in the breath between the strides.

Some of my best decisions haven't come from pushing harder, but from stopping just long enough to ask: Is this still right? Is this still me? And sometimes, the strongest move might not be to press forward, but to breathe, realign and begin again— not from obligation, but from a place that feels more honest.

Every year, I travel to one of the world's largest creative festivals. It's become a ritual of sorts; a pause that doesn't mean stopping, but stepping out of the everyday routine and environment. I spend a week surrounded by ideas, possibilities and people who see the world through a different lens. The conversations, the work and the sheer energy of it all shake patterns loose that I don't always notice in my day-to-day. It's a brilliant annual reset. Being in that environment helps me reflect on what we're doing, how we're doing it and where we might need to evolve. I often come home with renewed clarity because I switched context and found a new perspective.

I've also seen the power of pause play out in others. A regional CMO I knew was deeply unhappy in his role. On paper, everything looked perfect—senior title, broad scope, strong results—but he was exhausted and unfulfilled. He was moving at full speed, caught on the treadmill of achievement and fear and convinced that slowing down would mean failure. It took a health scare to stop him long enough to see what was happening. That enforced pause became the turning point that allowed him to reassess what mattered. He made deliberate changes and found a new role—one that gave him energy again. Today, he leads in a more balanced way, and often says he wishes he hadn't waited for a crisis to take a pause.

What this taught me is that pausing looks different for everyone. For some, it's an intentional step back. For others, it's a moment that life forces upon us. The wisdom lies in recognising the signs early and knowing that the pause is needed before it's demanded.

This is something I'm still learning and practising. There are weeks when the rhythm returns too quickly and the calendar overflows, the pace creeps back in and I forget. Until my body reminds me. Or I almost miss the question my son asks. Or I find myself staring at a screen, solving nothing. So I pause. Not for hours. Not always for days. But for long enough to remember that I have permission to stop for a moment, then re-engage with intention.

Sometimes that means taking time between flights, quite literally, to reflect on what's working and what isn't. Other times, it means shifting the scenery. Once, I chose to work from another country for a few weeks. I was still connected but surrounded by different sounds, light and people. That change of environment gave me a new perspective on challenges that had been too close to see clearly. It reminded me that rest doesn't always mean stopping; sometimes it just means stepping far enough away to see differently.

There's wisdom that comes from moments like these—that pausing isn't just for me, it's for the people I lead. When

I pause, I give them permission, too, to reflect, reset, and not pretend they have it all together all the time or have to keep sprinting to prove their value. That's how cultures shift: through leaders who show that space is productive, too. That ripple effect matters. It creates cultures where reflection is respected, presence is valued and humans are allowed to be... human.

If you're waiting for someone to grant you permission to pause, I want you to know that you don't have to earn it and you don't have to schedule a crisis to justify it. You only have to decide that your clarity, your energy and your presence are worth protecting. Because they are. And you are.

So I invite you to consider:

- Where have you been pushing forward on autopilot?

- What might change if you paused long enough to see clearly again?

- What would it take to give yourself full permission not to stop everything, but to stop for long enough to hear what your next step should really be?

- And how might you lead differently if you treated the pause not as a break from progress, but as the very thing that makes it possible?

17

Deciding
to Stay

THERE'S A NARRATIVE that's repeated often: that real growth requires leaving. Leaving the role, the company, the country, the comfort zone. We glorify the leap—whether it's a bold career change, a geographic relocation or a pivot into something unexpected. The story is told as one of courage, reinvention and forward motion. And sometimes, that story is exactly right.

But there's another version. One that is far less celebrated. That story is the decision to stay.

Deciding to stay doesn't always look like a win. It's not celebrated on LinkedIn or shared from conference stages, but in its own way, it can be every bit as brave as walking away.

Staying is often misunderstood. It can be misread as inertia, complacency or a lack of ambition. But sometimes, staying is a critically strategic, shrewdly intentional act. It's choosing to recommit to a challenge with eyes wide open. It's staying for the right reasons—not because it's easy, but because it's right.

In high-performance cultures, the instinct to move is strong. There is momentum and pressure, both internal and external, to constantly step up, out or on. But what if staying doesn't mean standing still? What if it means standing with a team, a purpose, or growth that hasn't reached its full expression?

This choice often emerges when everything is telling a leader to go. When frustrations mount. When politics get noisy. When the recognition feels uneven or the sacrifices start to feel personal. When the path ahead is unclear, the escape hatch can feel more attractive than the hard work of staying.

In those moments, the decision to stay can come from a place of deep alignment. It might be the subtle feeling that something important is being built. That timing matters. That not every exit is a step forward. That some challenges require resolve rather than reinvention.

Staying can build resilience. When a leader chooses to hold steady during a restructure, a downturn or a difficult transition, they learn what it means to lead without the usual validation. They build muscles for influence without authority, for creativity inside constraints, for empathy amid exhaustion.

A fellow CMO once confided that they wanted to take their brand in a direction that wasn't endorsed by the CEO and leadership team, and this was causing intense frustration. Around the same time, they were approached for another role, which looked easier, shinier and far more appealing. Yet they chose to stay. They stayed because they believed in the work, in the potential of the brand, and in what could still be achieved if they persisted. That decision paid off. In time, the CMO's persistence led to a shift in perspective across the leadership table, and the brand found its voice again. The outcome was better for the business, the brand and for him personally. And it was a testament to the power of staying when it truly matters.

I've had my own version of that story, too. Years ago, I found myself working for a CEO who created a toxic environment, where fear and ego crushed trust and collaboration. I could have left, and many did. But I made a conscious decision to stay long enough to protect my team, stabilise the brand, and ensure that the organisation would be stronger when I eventually walked away. It wasn't easy. It cost me energy, sleep, and no small amount of resilience. But when I did resign, my team was supported, the brand was in the best shape yet, and the CEO was removed by the board. Staying in that situation wasn't about endurance for its own sake, it was about stewardship. About leaving something in better shape than I found it, and knowing that, sometimes, integrity means finishing the hard chapters before you close the book.

The decision to stay isn't about self-sacrifice. It's not about being a martyr to a mission or tolerating the intolerable. It's about making a conscious choice to be in it; fully, responsibly and with purpose. It's about knowing your worth and choosing to stay because there is something here to be finished, to be fixed or to be fought for.

It's also about redefinition. Staying doesn't mean saying no to growth, but it might mean growing differently. Deepening skills instead of just expanding them. Cultivating influence rather than chasing status. Exploring new dimensions of leadership in the same context, rather than seeking novelty in a different one. It's growth that values maturity over motion.

This path can feel lonely, especially in a world that rewards visible milestones: the new job, the new title, the next big thing. But staying creates its own legacy. The leader who stays long enough to transform a culture, mentor the next wave, or drive real and lasting change makes contributions that can outlast the loudest exit.

There are, of course, risks in staying. The risk of stagnation. The risk of being taken for granted. The risk of becoming invisible in a system that values motion over meaning.

That's why intention is key. Staying well is not a passive mission. It requires boundaries, self-reflection and continuous recalibration. A thoughtful decision to stay includes questions like: What am I still learning here? What impact is still possible? What needs to evolve for this to remain fulfilling? How can I sustain both my energy and my influence?

Staying doesn't mean staying the same. It means evolving with awareness. It means adjusting expectations, creating internal momentum and finding micro-renewals in the everyday. It may mean renegotiating the role, the rhythm or the rewards. And it definitely means being honest—with yourself and others—about what is required to keep going.

There's real power in rewriting the narrative. What if the next chapter isn't somewhere else, but right here? What if the leader you're becoming is created not by the leap, but by the endurance and the steady, conscious act of staying and shaping from within? Instead of assuming that the right next thing is always elsewhere, consider that it might be right here.

Organisations benefit from those who stay with purpose. These leaders become institutional memory, cultural anchors and trusted stewards of change. But more than that, they model something vital: that growth is not always about what's next. Sometimes, it's about what's now.

In the end, both leaving and staying require courage, but they come from different muscles and perhaps it's time to give both their rightful place in the story.

So I invite you to consider:

- Where are you feeling pressure to leave because it's what's expected, not what's aligned?

- What would it mean to stay—on purpose and with purpose?

- And how might that staying become a deeper expression of your growth?

18

Weight
and Balance

BEFORE EVERY FLIGHT, there's a simple but essential calculation: weight and balance. It's what determines whether a plane can take off safely, stay in the air and land smoothly. It accounts for cargo, fuel, passengers, and even the way everything is distributed. It's not just about what's on board; it's about where and how it's held.

Leadership is much the same.

Over time, our roles accumulate weight. Projects, expectations, performance metrics, board reports, personal milestones, team dynamics, private griefs and public wins. Some of it we invite. Some of it is handed to us without warning. And some of it we don't even realise we're carrying until the strain shows up in unexpected ways—fatigue, doubt, burnout, restlessness.

When you've been leading for a while, the challenge isn't always about capability. It becomes about capacity. What are you carrying that no longer belongs to you? What have you taken on because no one else could—or would? What is essential to your journey now, and what is weighing you down?

We're not often encouraged to ask these questions. Especially in high-performing cultures, leadership can be measured by how much you can hold, not whether you're holding the right things. Endurance is praised. Busyness is mistaken for impact. And the cost? Invisible. Out of sight. But the most sustainable leaders I know don't just keep going, they choose to recalibrate. They might do this out of earshot, and it might be painful, but it's always done with intention.

I once sat down with a senior leader who described her calendar as an archaeological site. Every recurring meeting, every obligation, every time block was a layer of decisions made long ago, many of which no longer served her current role—or her future one. Her weight and balance were off, and she knew it. But awareness wasn't enough. It took courage to consciously realign by saying no, delegating, cancelling and protecting white space. She didn't just edit her calendar, she redefined what leadership meant.

And that's the thing: balance isn't static. What works at one altitude won't hold at another. The weight of a new strategy, a change in personal circumstances, or a shift in team dynamics requires leaders to recheck the distribution. Are we still leading in alignment with our purpose? Or are we just staying airborne on autopilot?

Sometimes, this recalibration reveals something surprising: that what we thought was essential... isn't. That an initiative we've poured months into needs to be shelved. That a relationship we've been holding together out of duty no longer creates mutual growth. That certain roles we've held—mentor, fixer, middle—need to evolve.

Other times, it confirms what we already know deep down: that space needs to be made for something new. A new ambition. A creative pursuit. A different rhythm. Or simply the permission to pause.

Weight and balance isn't about doing less for the sake of it. It's about leading well for longer. It's about checking that what you carry is what you need for your journey, and that the energy you're expending is connected to the impact you're trying to create.

And it's not just personal. Teams feel it too. When a leader is overloaded or out of balance, it ripples. It shows up in how decisions are made, how quickly burnout spreads, how safe it feels to speak up. Rebalancing isn't indulgent; it's responsible.

There's also the cultural weight we carry. The invisible load of being the only one, the first one, or the one expected to always have the answers. For many, the load is compounded by identity, past experiences and unspoken expectations. That weight doesn't appear on performance reviews, but it shapes how we land.

A friend once told me about a colleague who was the only woman in her regional leadership team. She didn't just carry her own workload, she carried representation. Every meeting, every decision, every visible moment felt like it had to prove something bigger than herself. When she began mentoring others and building a more diverse bench of leaders, she realised that she didn't need to carry it all alone. By sharing the weight, she multiplied the impact and created space for others to rise beside her, not behind her.

Sometimes we stay in the air for so long, holding everything and everyone else up, that we forget to check in on ourselves. That's when things slip. It starts slowly. The joy starts to dull. We feel less certain. The clarity blurs. And by the time we notice it, we're already off course.

I've had moments when I realised that what I was carrying wasn't heavy because it was important, but because I hadn't set it down in years. Taking time between flights, or working from a different environment, is one way I can rebalance and change the view just long enough to see what really matters.

This is the invitation: not to drop everything, but to reweigh and rebalance. Rebalancing might look like shifting a strategic priority or taking a proper break without guilt. It might mean asking for help. It might mean letting go of a task you've always done because someone else can now take it further. It might mean saying something out loud that you've been holding in.

There is no perfect formula. But there is a mindset: that leadership is not just about staying aloft, but staying aligned. Not just about capacity, but clarity. Not just about doing it all, but doing what matters.

Every flight checks its weight and balance before taking off. Maybe it's time we did the same.

So I invite you to consider:

- What are you carrying that no longer serves you or your work?

- Where might you need to redistribute the weight—within your team, your priorities or yourself?

- What needs to shift for you to lead with greater balance and purpose?

- And how might rebalancing now give you the lift you need for the journey ahead?

19

Holding Pattern

THERE'S A POINT in air travel where the plane is so close to landing that you can see the destination below. The lights. The roads. A landscape you recognise. And yet, instead of descending, the plane circles.

This is a holding pattern.

It's not a delay due to failure. It's not an error. It's often a deliberate choice; a signal that conditions aren't quite right to land. Sometimes it's weather. Sometimes it's traffic. Sometimes the runway isn't ready.

Leadership has holding patterns, too.

There are times when we know where we're headed. We've done the prep. We're ready. We can see the runway coming into view. But something in the environment says, 'Not yet.' And so we circle. We hover just above the outcome, caught between readiness and restraint.

We don't always talk about these seasons. They don't look like high growth or major change. They don't feel unusually exciting. But they test us. Because modern leadership culture tells us that momentum equals progress. That visibility equals impact. That landing the next big thing is what shows your value.

But holding patterns challenge that narrative. They ask us to wait without losing clarity and remain calm without growing passive. To stay engaged, even when we can't detect any forward motion.

Sometimes the hardest move is the one you hold back. I remember leading a major rebrand that entailed months of groundwork. The creative was ready, the team was energised and the appetite for launch was high. But the timing wasn't right. Market sentiment was shifting and the business context was unstable. It took restraint to pause when everything in me wanted to move. But that delay made the difference. When we did launch, the work landed with greater clarity, confidence and impact.

Waiting is not easy, especially for leaders wired for delivery. Those are the kind of leaders who pride themselves on execution and who have built reputations on being the ones who land the plane, no matter how bad the weather.

But the truth is that some of the wisest decisions come from waiting. From sensing that now isn't the moment to force a move. That landing too early could cause more damage than good. That growth, sometimes, needs more airspace and pushing through isn't always the same as pushing forward.

Waiting doesn't mean disengaging. In fact, holding patterns can be some of the most focused periods of leadership. They require close attention. Active listening. A strategic lens. A readiness to act as soon as the green light appears.

And they often reveal more than we expect.

Because in the absence of fast outcomes, we get a clearer look at our instincts and our relationship with control. We learn whether we trust ourselves when the pace slows. And whether we can hold space for others who are navigating their own uncertainty, without rushing to provide answers we don't yet have. Some leaders fill the holding pattern with noise. They micromanage. They overcorrect. They confuse activity with progress. But the most grounded leaders learn to observe, calibrate and ask better questions. To tend to what often gets overlooked in faster seasons: team health, creative capacity, quiet culture shifts and the inner dialogue that shapes how we show up.

A regional managing director once told me that when their business hit a six-month strategic pause during a merger, the hardest part wasn't managing the uncertainty—it was resisting the urge to overfill the space. They focused instead on team wellbeing, one-to-one conversations and reinforcing culture. By the time the new direction was confirmed, the team was stronger, more connected and ready to move together. The waiting became its own form of progress.

There's real power in being able to say: we are circling right now, and that is okay. It gives your team permission to be human and acknowledge that progress doesn't always look like landing a new strategy. Sometimes it looks like readiness and discipline. Like not forcing the story to end before it's ready to be told.

In my experience, holding patterns often appear in leadership right before a major shift, a restructure or a reinvention. They signal a renewal of purpose. Those leaders who rush through miss the nuance and can react instead of respond. They land too soon and burn out on the runway.

And those who wait with intention? They land with clarity and alignment. With integrity still intact.

This doesn't mean we should avoid decisions or abdicate leadership. It means we make space for decisions to be better informed. For the context to evolve. For others to catch up. For timing to serve the outcome instead of undermining it.

The hardest part is sitting with the discomfort of the pause, especially when others are watching and want certainty. When they're looking to you for pace progress and for plans. But leadership isn't always about speed. It's also about sensing, timing, awareness.

If you're in a holding pattern right now, ask yourself: What is this space offering me? What can I see from this vantage point that I might miss at ground level? What clarity is forming beneath the stillness? Because stillness is not the same as stagnation. Holding patterns often birth the most strategic pivots, the most resilient teams and the most creative breakthroughs. But only if we honour them as a phase with value, not a lull to be tolerated.

Not every flight lands on schedule. Not every outcome needs to arrive on our preferred timeline. But when we stop circling just because we're impatient, and instead land because the moment is truly right, we lead from a different place.

One that blends readiness with wisdom. Action with timing. Urgency with trust.

So I invite you to consider:

- Where in your leadership are you being asked to wait, and what might that waiting be preparing you for?

- How do you tend to react to delays and what would intentional waiting look like?

- What could become clearer if you gave this holding pattern a little more space?

20

Light at
Low Battery

BURNOUT ISN'T ALWAYS a dramatic crash. For many, it's quiet. Lingering. Ongoing. It's the heaviness that creeps in when your calendar is full, your tank is low and your spark is harder to ignite. And for those carrying a lot—at work, at home and in between—that feeling might not be temporary. It can become a constant undercurrent.

In recent months, I've had countless conversations with leaders across industries, countries and contexts, and the pattern is unmistakable. Many of them are carrying a kind of burnout that doesn't flare and fade, but smoulders among the embers.

It's not a crisis anymore. It's a condition. A constant, low-grade depletion that we've somehow learnt to survive with.

We might check in on each other and share small coping strategies, but we rarely talk about changing the system because, truthfully, most of us feel we can't. There's empathy in those conversations, but also resignation. The state of the workplace, the expectations, the pace; they're not designed for rest. And while we might find pockets of relief, the deeper shift so many of us crave feels impossibly out of reach.

But what I've come to understand is that preventing burn-out, or even just managing the weight of it, doesn't always require a full reset.

Sometimes, it starts with something small but intentional—better working rhythms and micro-moments that can shift your energy. A fifteen-minute moment of joy—not productivity, not progress—just joy, as you define it.

Whether you're working from home or in the office, these moments matter. Cuddles with a pet. A walk around the block. Journaling a stray thought. A coffee run with a colleague who makes you laugh. A chat in the hallway that unexpectedly lifts your mood. Dancing around the living room like no one's watching (because no one is). Stepping outside between meetings to feel the sun on your face. Or simply closing your laptop, putting your phone down, and letting your mind wander for a few minutes; no guilt attached.

These tiny moments don't solve everything, but they soften the edges. They remind your nervous system that not every second has to be a sprint. They let the light back in. And they've taught me that small shifts in how we move through the day can make a big difference.

Over time, I've realised that how I structure my day can shape how I feel. I call it diary design. And it's the simple practice of shaping your day with intention—not perfection, but purpose. Being mindful of not just what fills your calendar, but who. It's about planning moments with the people who bring clarity, humour or encouragement, especially when part of your day includes conversations that can drain or deplete you. Placing energising interactions between the heavier ones lets them act like buffers for your nervous system. Try scheduling ten minutes after a big meeting to give you time to reflect, instead of rushing into the next one. Or blocking space not just to catch up, but to catch your breath.

It's about treating your calendar not just as a schedule, but as a source of energy. And while it doesn't always go to plan, on the days it does, you really feel it. These aren't grand strategies, but they help. And sometimes, help is enough. It's not always perfect. But it's real. And it's me.

Moments between flights are where I sometimes reconnect with these small but essential reminders. Because it's not always about slowing down. It's about finding ways to keep going with energy, with grace and with yourself intact.

So I invite you to consider:

- Where are the micro-moments in your day that help you breathe, think or simply be?

- What's one way you could design your time to protect your energy—not just your schedule?

- Who helps you feel most like yourself again when the pace picks up?

21

Back to
What Matters

VERY SO OFTEN, leadership asks us to return to what's essential. Not the newest framework or strategy, but the principles that hold everything together and the values that don't expire when trends change. Things like trust, respect, presence and gratitude. These are not soft skills; they're stabilising forces. They remind us that leadership is not just about outcomes, but about the tone we set and the energy we bring.

For me, gratitude has always been one of those principles. It's not just something I say, but something I do. I start meetings with it. I end conversations with it. I make sure people know where they've added value; to the work, to the day, to the energy around us. It's not about being nice. It's about being intentional. When someone feels seen, when they know their effort meant something, it builds connection. And that connection is what lasts.

I remember a workshop where the facilitator paused mid-discussion to thank someone who had quietly solved a problem that no one else had noticed. The recognition took less than a minute, yet the whole room lifted. You could feel the energy shift. Gratitude changes atmosphere.

I'm not talking about surface-level appreciation. I mean real, grounded gratitude; the kind that recognises what's often invisible—the long hours, the steady holding together. The person who made something better without asking for credit.

Gratitude is more than a feel-good habit; it shapes culture. It creates rhythm. It tells people, 'I see you, and this matters.' And lately, I keep coming back to the same question: What still matters?

In the rush of transformation and the noise about what's next, it's easy to lose sight of the things that have always grounded good leadership. Not in a nostalgic way, but with clarity and steadiness. Because while business evolves and organisations pivot, some things stay constant. Those things aren't trendy or loud, but they are essential.

Trust is one of those things. Not just brand trust, but the human kind. The kind that's earned slowly and protected carefully. It's in the people who do what they said they would. Who follow through and create the safety for others to stretch, speak up, or admit they don't have it all figured out. I once worked with a leader who never promised more than she could deliver, and when she said, 'Leave it with me,' everyone knew it would be done. That reliability built confidence across the team. In a fast-moving world, trust steadies the ground beneath us.

And when everything is moving, clarity helps too. It doesn't mean having all the answers. It means naming what matters most so people don't waste energy chasing the wrong things. The best leaders I've worked with—and the version of myself I try to bring to work—weren't always certain, but they were clear. That clarity helps people focus. I had a senior colleague who once drew a circle around a single word on a whiteboard and said, 'This is our priority. Everything else is noise.' It wasn't profound, but it brought instant calm to a tense room. Clarity has that effect. In a distracted world, focus becomes a kind of superpower.

Respect matters too. Not formality or hierarchy, but the everyday kind; how we run meetings, how we handle feedback, how we disagree without dismantling someone's confidence. It doesn't take much to offer, but it costs a lot when it's missing. One day I watched a leader handle a heated debate by simply saying, 'Let's pause; we're not listening to each other yet.' The room exhaled. It wasn't about control; it was about care. Respect makes people lean in and its absence makes them withdraw.

Then there's presence. The real kind. Not just sitting in the meeting, but being in it. Presence that listens all the way through. That notices when someone's holding back and asks the second question, not just the polite one.

I once watched a CEO during a tense meeting close her laptop and look around the table. The room went still. Then she said, 'Tell me what you're not saying.' The tension broke and was replaced by honesty. Presence can shift a room faster than authority ever will.

Consistency might not sound exciting, but it might be one of the most powerful qualities a leader can offer. Not just consistency in messaging, but in behaviour. How we show up on the hard days. How we make decisions when no one's watching. How our values appear not just in strategy decks, but in trade-offs and conversations. People don't need perfection; they need something they can believe in. I admire a colleague whose reaction never changes, no matter how high the stakes are. That steadiness makes people brave enough to break bad news early, not hide it. Consistency builds trust long before a title does.

And then there's energy. Not the performative kind, but the kind that sustains. Leadership is a transfer of energy. You can feel it the moment someone walks into a room—are they calm or chaotic, grounded or reactive? That tone sets the tempo for everyone else. I've learnt to manage my own battery not just for myself, but for the people who rely on me to be steady, focused and real. On the days when I arrive depleted, I can see how quickly it ripples through a team. Energy sets culture more than words ever can.

None of these are new ideas. But when things feel off or when morale dips or creativity stalls, it's rarely because something new is missing. It's usually because we've lost touch with something foundational.

Returning to what matters reminds me of the kind of leader I want to be. That's the kind who listens. Who notices. Who creates space for others to step into their best. The kind who doesn't just chase the next thing, but builds on something that lasts.

The future will always demand fresh thinking; that's the work. But the ideas that really land—the ones people remember—are built on something steady and human.

So I invite you to consider:

- What are the values and behaviours that hold your team together?

- Are you modelling what you say you care about, or only naming it?

- Are you creating a culture where these anchors are lived, or leaving them to chance?

- The future of work will always evolve, but leadership that lasts is built on what we choose to keep.

22

The Leadership
of Patience

T HERE COMES A POINT in leadership when the questions start to shift. It's less about *what comes next* and more about *how you move through now.* It's not just what you achieve, but how you pace yourself in pursuit of it. The longer you lead, the more you realise that progress isn't only about motion, it's about momentum, timing and trust.

Patience, for me, has never come naturally.

I like momentum. I like action. I like it when things move. And in the pace of high-performance environments, impatience doesn't always look like a flaw. It looks like drive. It sounds like urgency. It gets packaged as ambition. And there have been many moments when it has served me well.

But I've also learnt that impatience, when it goes unchecked, can pull you away from the leader you're trying to be.

Impatience shows up as frustration when change doesn't come fast enough. As restlessness when the results don't match the effort. As a silent desire for recognition when the impact is real, but invisible. It can make you want to fix, to jump in, to push. And in doing so, it can cloud your intention. It can turn long-term thinking into short-term problem-solving and legacy into something we chase, rather than something we build.

But learning to lead with patience isn't about slowing everything down. It's about choosing when to move and when to wait. About knowing that impact isn't always immediate, and what you seed today might take years to show results—and that's okay. The most meaningful outcomes often take time to reveal themselves. Sometimes months. Sometimes years.

I've learnt this from the people I've led and the work I've left behind, but also through the times when my patience was most tested.

I once led a cross-regional initiative that I believed in deeply. After months of strategy sessions, alignment meetings and careful groundwork, the rollout was delayed. For weeks, I felt restless and feared we were losing momentum. But the pause turned out to be pivotal. It created space for stronger buy-in, deeper collaboration and a far more sustainable result. It reminded me that patience isn't absence of action— it's intelligent timing.

The fact is, most of us learn patience the hard way. Especially those of us who are used to leading from the front. There's always that inner pull to close the gap, tidy the edges and keep moving at pace. But I've learnt to pause long enough to ask: Is this about what needs to be done, or about my need to be the one doing it? That single question changes everything.

Sometimes the most generous act of leadership is restraint. Holding back to let someone else rise. Trusting that their way might look different from yours—and that's not just acceptable, it's necessary.

The leaders I've admired most have all shared one trait: composure in uncertainty. They didn't fill silence with noise. They didn't rush to prove their worth. They trusted timing, and in doing so, built it.

I have a colleague who once led a high-stakes merger integration where everyone wanted rapid results. Instead of forcing change, she slowed the process and focused first on rebuilding trust across teams. It was uncomfortable for stakeholders who wanted instant proof of progress, but it paid off. The integration succeeded because people were ready for it, not rushed into it. Patience didn't stall progress; it enabled it.

And it's not easy. When you care deeply, when you're across every detail, letting go feels risky. But patience is not passivity—it's perspective. It's the willingness to step back just enough for others to step in.

Impatience still visits me, of course. There are days when I want to move faster, fix more, see progress now. But those are the moments when I breathe before acting. I remind myself that visibility isn't proof of impact, and speed isn't the same as success.

Leading with patience requires intention. It's the discipline of zooming out and playing the long game. It's not about being everywhere fast; it's about being exactly where you need to be at the right time and at the right pace. That's where peace lives, too. When you release the need to hold everything tightly and move everything forward at speed, you create space for others to rise. What lasts isn't the noise of achievement, but the steadiness and calm you model along the way.

So I invite you to consider:

- Where has impatience been shaping your leadership, and what might patience make possible instead?

- What's one decision you could hold a little longer to make it stronger?

- How might slowing your pace help others find theirs?

23

Leading Without the Mask

HERE'S A CERTAIN version of ourselves we learn to wear at work, especially in leadership. The version that is composed. Certain. In control. The version that knows how to answer, manage, plan and inspire. It's not dishonest. It's just curated. And over time, that mask becomes so familiar that we sometimes forget that we're wearing it.

When I first stepped into leadership, I thought this was how it had to be. I thought my team needed to see strength— always. That any crack in the façade would erode trust or weaken my credibility. So I learnt to show the version of myself that was expected. That was a leader with the right answers. The one who kept things moving, no matter what was happening underneath the surface.

But the older I get, in life and in leadership, the more I crave the kind of presence that doesn't have to be performed. The kind where you can exhale and show up as the full version of yourself, not just the polished outline. Because real connection does not come from polish. It comes from honesty, humanity and being the kind of leader who can say, 'I do not have all the answers', 'I am still figuring it out' and 'This one is hard for me too'.

I have found that the strongest leaders I know are not always the most confident. But they are the most grounded. They're not trying to impress. But they are trying to connect. They're not the loudest voice in the room, but the clearest one. And they know that vulnerability, when used with intention, is not weakness; it's strength.

Of course, there is wisdom in discernment. Not every room is safe, and not every moment calls for vulnerability. There are times when you need to hold it together, even when you're crumbling inside. Times when leadership asks you to steady the room before you steady yourself. Times when the mask is not performance, but protection.

But too much masking, for too long, creates a different kind of fatigue. The kind that disconnects you from yourself and leaves you lying awake at night, wondering who you are when no one is watching. And in leadership, that disconnection trickles down. It shapes culture and trust. It teaches others that strength means silence, that confidence means pretending and that leadership means being untouchable.

I remember a conversation with a team member from years ago. She told me, quietly, that she had been scared to admit she was struggling because 'you always seem to have it together'. It was meant as a compliment, but it landed heavily. I realised that my mask—albeit unintentionally—had created distance. It had made it harder for her to share her own challenges because she thought she had to match the version of leadership she saw in me.

That was a turning point. It reminded me that when leaders hide too much, they make it harder for others to be honest. And when we lead from a place of perfection, we inadvertently teach our teams to do the same.

The truth is, the leaders I have admired most were never untouchable; they were human. They showed their care. They admitted when things were hard. They asked questions they did not know the answers to. They led with honesty, not armour.

One leader stands out in my memory. She was brilliant, composed and respected. But what made her unforgettable was the way she would pause in a meeting and say, 'I don't know. What do you think?' It wasn't a tactic or a performance. She asked the question because she genuinely valued the perspectives around her. That single act of humility created space for others to step in, to think boldly, to lead alongside her. And it reminded me that leadership is not about being the smartest in the room. It's about creating rooms where others feel smart enough to speak.

When we lead without the mask, carefully but courageously, we create more human workplaces. More honest teams. More room to breathe. And often, we find that we are not just leading others more authentically, we are finally meeting ourselves, too.

This doesn't mean we abandon boundaries. There is a difference between honesty and oversharing. Between being real and being raw. Leading without the mask is not about dumping every thought or fear on your team. It's about showing up with integrity and letting people see enough of the truth to trust you, without expecting them to carry your load. It also asks us to notice where the mask is serving us, and where it is hiding us.

Sometimes, the mask gives us courage to step into a moment we are not ready for. Sometimes, it buys us the time we need to find our footing. But if it becomes the only version we show, we risk losing sight of the leader underneath.

When you let the mask slip, a different kind of energy is released. Conversations become easier. Feedback becomes richer. People stop posturing and start collaborating. The room feels lighter because no one is carrying the weight of pretending. And yes, it takes courage to go first. It takes courage to say, 'I need help.' To admit you are learning. To own the fact that leadership is hard sometimes.

But that courage is contagious. It gives your team permission to be real, too. And in that space, trust grows. Creativity flows and people feel safe enough to bring their full selves to the work.

When I think back to the moments I am most proud of as a leader, they were not the ones when I was perfectly polished. They were the moments when I showed up real. The times when I said, 'This is hard, but we will get through it together.' The conversations where I admitted I had got it wrong, and asked how to make it right. The quiet check-ins where I told someone, 'I see you.'

Those are the moments that stick with you. Not because they were flawless, but because they were human.

So if you have been holding the mask a little too tightly, maybe this is your reminder to loosen the grip. To let yourself be seen, not just as the leader with the answers, but as the person asking the questions. To choose presence over performance. To show your team that strength does not mean being untouchable, it means being trustworthy. Because the legacy we leave is not built on how perfectly we played the part, but on how fully we showed up.

So I invite you to consider:

- Where are you still wearing a version of yourself that no longer feels true?

- What would shift if you led with honesty, rather than armour?

- And how might your team, and you, breathe easier if you allowed the mask to come off, even just a little?

24

The Space
to Become

SOMETIMES, BETWEEN FLIGHTS, you find yourself in transit, suspended between destinations, waiting to move forward. You're no longer where you were, but not yet where you're going. It's a space that can feel uncertain and uncomfortable. But, like in our careers, those in-between moments often hold the most meaningful kind of growth. Because transition, like transit, isn't about standing still; it's about preparing to move differently.

And just like travel, some seasons of life whisper that change is coming before we can name what it is. You can feel it before you can define it; a budding restlessness, a tug that something no longer fits. It isn't failure. It's evolution. For many of us, this shows up most clearly in our work. *The space to become* is the stretch between chapters; that uncertain middle where one role, identity or rhythm is ending, but the next hasn't yet begun.

I used to think progress was about staying in motion; about always knowing the next goal, the next title, the next project.

Success was a sequence of arrivals. But there comes a point when momentum alone no longer feels like meaning. You start to sense that what once energised you now drains you, or that you've outgrown the role you're in or the version of yourself it requires.

Growth isn't just about speed, it's about alignment. It's about recognising when the career you built no longer reflects the person you're becoming. That realisation rarely arrives gently. It can feel disorienting, even guilt-inducing, especially when everything looks successful from the outside. But that discomfort is often the first signal of transformation.

This phase is messy. It's not when you announce a bold new direction or celebrate a milestone. It's the liminal middle where things are still forming. You may not know what you want yet—you only know it's not this. But that's exactly where the work begins. Real evolution often hides inside uncertainty.

For leaders, career transitions are particularly confronting. We're trained to be decisive, productive, clear. But sometimes, the bravest thing you can do is admit you don't know yet. Because not knowing is where reinvention begins. Every meaningful pivot starts as a pause you didn't plan.

I've been there myself. There was a time when my title looked strong on paper, but inside, I was unfulfilled. The role was still demanding, still respected, but it no longer aligned with my curiosity or values. I knew I needed change, but I didn't know what that change was. That gap between awareness and clarity is what this space is about. Looking back, those were the times that reshaped me most profoundly. I began exploring small experiments, saying yes to projects that stretched me in new ways, mentoring outside my company and reconnecting with creative work that used to light me up. None of it was part of a grand plan. But each step helped me rediscover what energised me.

Transitions often feel like freefall. You've let go of the old, but the new hasn't appeared. You question your timing, your value, your direction. But that space isn't wasted; it's where identity realigns with purpose. It's the necessary quiet before clarity takes shape.

The world doesn't reward this kind of transition. It rewards the visible kind: new jobs, bold announcements, neat story arcs. But most career evolution happens quietly. Without LinkedIn updates. Without titles. Without anyone clapping. It's not about being seen; it's about becoming ready.

It happens when you start listening differently to your energy, your curiosity, your exhaustion. When you stop filling every space with productivity and start asking: What does 'enough' really mean now?

I can think of one year when I was doing everything right— delivering results, leading teams, earning recognition—but inside, I knew I was done. Because I'd grown past what the role could teach me. It took months of listening, journaling and uncomfortable stillness before I could articulate what was next. That process didn't just change my job, it changed how I made decisions.

Sometimes we don't choose the transition—life does. I've seen leaders face redundancy, restructure or burnout that forced them into reflection. One former colleague described it as being 'pushed off a moving train.' But as she rebuilt, slowly, she discovered that freedom can begin where certainty ends. That space between the old and the unknown is confronting, but it's also clarifying. It strips away the noise and helps you remember what matters. Who you are without the brand name, the title or the next meeting in your diary.

We need to normalise these career thresholds. They're not derailments; they're recalibrations. They signal readiness for what's next, even if you can't name it. As leaders, we often don't give ourselves permission to pause between chapters. We fear it'll look like weakness or indecision. But the truth is, clarity doesn't arrive on command. It emerges slowly, like dawn—you barely notice it until, suddenly, the next horizon is visible.

Becoming requires trust, especially in moments of career transition. Trust that the reflection will become direction. That what feels uncertain today is shaping tomorrow. That the space you're standing in isn't empty, it's an active part of your evolution. It's not wasted time—it's preparation time.

For me, it's meant learning to sit in that in-between and resisting the urge to fill every gap with a new role, a new title or a new plan. To let curiosity lead before clarity arrives. Because growth doesn't always begin with certainty. It often begins with a question: What if there's another way to do this? What if there's another version of me still waiting to be expressed?

There have been times when I felt like I was standing on a bridge between two worlds: the career I'd built and the one

I hadn't yet imagined. The temptation to rush across was strong. But staying long enough to really understand what was ending, and what I wanted next, changed everything. It made the eventual move more deliberate, more aligned and ultimately more sustainable.

I've seen this play out many times with others too. I know a leader who took six months out between senior roles, and used that space to explore the kind of work that truly energised her. She spent time mentoring, reconnecting with peers and exploring industries she'd never worked in. What she discovered wasn't just a new job, it was a new sense of purpose. She realised that the role she needed next wasn't the one that looked best on paper, but the one that best aligned with her values and energy.

That's the real work of becoming. It's not just about moving on, it's about moving with intention. It's about giving yourself the space to listen for what's next, even when everyone else expects you to already know.

And it's not always easy. There's grief in it too—grief for the version of yourself you're leaving behind, the routine that once felt like home, the recognition that used to define you.

But there's also renewal. Because every time we step into the unknown, we make space for something new to take root.

The space to become isn't about slowing down for the sake of rest. It's about slowing down long enough to realign and choose the next chapter consciously, not by default. So if you find yourself between roles, between identities, or simply between definitions of success, know that you're not behind. You're becoming. And that space you're in right now? That's where the future starts to take shape.

So I invite you to consider:

- Is there a part of your work or identity that you've out-grown, even if you haven't yet named what comes next?

- What might open up if you stopped rushing to fill the space between roles or seasons?

- And what if the version of you you're becoming is not waiting at the finish line, but already forming here, in this in-between?

25

The Power
of No

THERE'S A REAL strength in knowing when to say no. Not from avoidance or fear, but from clarity. That type of 'no' is a boundary that protects what matters most. It might be no to the extra call when you're already stretched. No to the opportunity that doesn't align with your values. No to the pace that keeps you moving but not thinking.

It doesn't always feel easy, especially when you care deeply, and when you want to show up, contribute and be helpful. But over time, I've learnt that no is a complete sentence that doesn't require guilt, justification or a spreadsheet of explanations. No isn't rejection. It's redirection. It's a decision to honour your energy, your focus and your time.

And sometimes, saying no is exactly what allows you to say yes. Yes to something that's quietly essential. Yes to your child. Yes to a creative spark. Yes to rest, reflection and the ideas that need space to land.

Because saying no isn't about shutting doors—it's about keeping the right ones open. But I also recognise that saying no doesn't come easily to everyone. For many, it brings up discomfort, fear of judgement or a sense of guilt. We've been conditioned to believe that being helpful means always being available, and that saying yes is the path to opportunity or approval.

Sometimes, it's more than a habit. It's an identity. Especially for those of us who've been praised for being agreeable, going the extra mile or being the one who says yes. Saying no can feel like letting someone down, or even letting go of a version of ourselves that once felt safe or admired.

There's also a cultural component. In many teams, saying yes is rewarded—quickly, visibly and often. But those gently defiant moments of discernment, when someone chooses what not to take on, don't get the same recognition, despite being just as vital. Behind every strategic yes is usually a thoughtful no.

But here's something I've learnt: you don't have to earn your boundaries. It's okay to pause before saying yes. To ask yourself: Does this align with what I value? Do I have the energy to do this well? Is this mine to carry?

Those pauses are where discernment grows. Another hard lesson I've learnt is that sometimes you have to say no to something good, not because it's unworthy, but because your energy is finite and your purpose deserves protection.

That kind of no isn't a rejection of the opportunity. It's a recommitment to what matters most.

Learning to say no doesn't require a dramatic declaration. Start small. Say no to things that drain your time without adding meaning. Replace the automatic yes with 'Let me check and get back to you.' Give yourself space to choose, not react. With each intentional no, clarity grows. So does confidence.

And sometimes, the best no is the one that's never heard. It's the one that lives in your calendar as protected time, that shows up in a declined meeting that lets you walk your child to school, or the boundary that simply isn't up for debate. These aren't signs of being difficult. They're signs of being deliberate.

And when you model that kind of clarity as a leader, you give others permission to do the same. Especially for people at the start of their careers, seeing a leader say no, with care and confidence, can be a powerful example.

I worked with a senior executive who had reached burnout from constantly saying yes. After taking a month off, she returned with a rule: one no for every new yes. Her impact deepened, her team's autonomy grew, and her reputation for clarity became one of her greatest strengths. Boundaries, she realised, weren't barriers—they were keys to better leadership.

I also remember a time, years ago, when a colleague asked for support on something that was absolutely fair, but not urgent or aligned with our top priorities. I felt the familiar pull to say yes and be helpful. But instead, I paused, and I said no. Not harshly, just honestly. I was surprised by what happened next. That 'no' gave me the space to offer something even more valuable to that same colleague a week later, something that truly made a difference to their work.

And in doing so, I realised that, sometimes, saying no in the moment opens the door to a better, future yes.

Leadership without boundaries is rarely sustainable. And generosity without limits can lead to depletion. When you say no with purpose you're not letting people down, you're setting a standard for the kind of leadership you want to model. Leadership that's rooted in clarity, not constant availability. In presence, not performance. In protecting your capacity so that when you do say yes, it's wholehearted, not half-drained.

One of the most powerful ways to support your team is to normalise saying no to the non-essential. If everything is a priority, nothing is. And when leaders make those distinctions clear, the team feels safer doing the same. You start to create a culture that values discernment over busyness. It also creates space for more meaningful moments of yes—the kind that reflect not just commitment, but connection. Saying yes to the project that lights someone up. Saying yes to rest that fuels the next breakthrough. Saying yes to yourself when the world expects more than you can give.

Taking some time to find a space where you can find that perspective again is important; when you're not yet in the next thing, but can hear what you need most. Saying no isn't the end of the conversation. It's the beginning of alignment.

So I invite you to consider:

- What request have you said yes to that's been weighing on you?

- Where could one small no create space for a more meaningful yes?

- How might you honour your capacity this week, without apology or guilt?

26

The Art of
Expecting Less

THERE ARE MOMENTS in leadership and in life when you realise that not everyone operates with the same intention or follow-through. Some people will arrive late, miss deadlines, or simply not do what they said they would.

I had a colleague who promised a key deliverable for a major presentation, then didn't show up. In the past, I would have spent hours feeling frustrated and trying to fix the situation while silently questioning their professionalism. But that day, I just opened my laptop, rebuilt the deck and delivered it myself. Not because I wasn't disappointed, but because staying upset wouldn't change the outcome. It would only drain me.

That experience taught me something liberating: when you start *expecting* people to be who they are, rather than who you wish they'd be, your peace returns.

It's not cynicism; it's clarity.

When you expect the person who always runs late to run late, you stop watching the clock. You make the coffee, take a breath and start the meeting when it's time. I once worked with a senior executive known for being late to every meeting. One of his team members finally stopped fighting it; she would schedule him for 9:00, knowing he'd arrive by 9:20, and used the first twenty minutes to connect with the rest of the group. What could have been wasted irritation turned into valuable team time. When you expect the person who overpromises to underdeliver, you plan for it. And when they surprise you by doing what they said they would, it's a pleasant bonus.

The beauty of this mindset is that it removes the sting. Disappointment is the gap between expectation and reality, and when you close that gap, you stop wasting emotional energy on what you can't control. You stop trying to reform other people's behaviour and instead reclaim your own equilibrium.

I see this lesson play out often in my teams. Someone will come to me exasperated because another person hasn't delivered what was promised. I can see the frustration on their face, the tension in their shoulders. In those moments, I encourage them to pause and see the choice we all have. We can get upset with the person who's let us down and replay the unfairness of it and question why others don't carry the same sense of responsibility. Or we can accept that this is who they are, expect the pattern to repeat, and focus instead on what we can do to achieve the outcome we want.

This can feel especially hard in high-pressure environments, where everyone is working long hours and the stakes are high. The gap between your level of effort and someone else's can feel almost offensive; how can they not see what's at stake? But that's the moment when emotional discipline matters most. Because frustration in those situations rarely fuels progress. In fact, it only amplifies exhaustion.

For many people, that shift feels hard at first. It can stir feelings of injustice and disappointment. It can make you feel exhausted, especially when the same people let you down repeatedly. But when you recognise that those emotions, while valid, don't serve you, you start to reclaim control. You realise the goal isn't to fix the other person, it's to free yourself from the frustration that comes from expecting something different. Over time, that awareness builds a calm strength—the kind that lets you move forward without resentment, that's grounded in clarity rather than reaction.

Of course, I understand not everyone will agree with this approach.

Some people feel compelled to address poor behaviour head-on; to make a point, call it out and drive accountability. And that's absolutely right when the person is in your team, because performance and standards must be managed directly. But what I'm talking about here are the people outside your team. Those are people you can influence, but not control. In those cases, spending your energy on confrontation rarely changes the outcome. I've learnt that holding calm boundaries and focusing on what you can do instead is often far more effective, and infinitely better for your wellbeing.

This isn't about lowering standards, it's about protecting your energy. It's about accepting that not everyone has your sense of urgency, ownership or care, and that's okay. The world needs all types, even if some make our days more complicated.

I think of it like inflight turbulence. You can't control when it happens, but you can choose how to ride it. You tighten your seatbelt, settle in and keep reading your book. You don't get angry at the wind.

These days, when someone doesn't do what they said they'd do, I don't give it the same weight. I note it, adjust and move forward. Because getting upset won't make them change but expecting them to be who they've shown you they are allows you to stay calm, stay grounded and keep flying at your own altitude.

And when I see others learning to do the same—to breathe, reset and move on—I'm reminded that calm can be contagious. Leadership isn't about absorbing everyone's frustration, it's about showing them there's another way to fly. There's a simple form of freedom in that. The freedom to keep your focus on what matters and let the rest drift by like clouds beneath you.

So I invite you to consider:

- Where in your world are you expecting someone to behave differently than they always have?

- And what might it look like to free yourself from that expectation, not to give up on them, but to give back to yourself?

27

Flight Plan, Revised

THERE'S COMFORT in having a plan. It provides structure, direction and a sense of control. For leaders, plans can feel like proof of progress: the five-year vision, the quarterly roadmap, the perfectly colour-coded calendar. Plans signal clarity to others. But what happens when the plan no longer fits? When the structure that once grounded you begins to feel like a cage?

Many of us begin our careers with a clear trajectory: milestones are mapped, ambitions are defined and success is measured by speed and scale. But somewhere along the way, life intervenes. Markets change overnight. A global pandemic rewrites business models. New technologies upend what once felt certain. Or perhaps there's a personal shift: a family change, a health scare, a move that forces a different view of what matters. Suddenly, the plan that once felt right starts to feel outdated. Not wrong, just no longer relevant. But this isn't failure. It's flight.

Because in aviation, even the best-filed flight plans change. Conditions shift mid-air—weather, turbulence, air traffic, tailwinds—and pilots adjust course. Flight plans are written with the assumption they'll need revision. Yet in leadership, we resist this truth. We cling to the original path even when the data, or our instincts, tell us otherwise.

Revising a flight plan isn't just a response to what's happening externally, it can be a response to what's changing internally. A quiet realisation that the role we once fought for no longer excites us. That the definition of success we built our careers around has shifted. That the life and leadership we want now need a new map.

Usually, the hardest part isn't the strategy, but the emotion.

Changing course can feel like failure, like letting people down, like admitting we were wrong. But what if it's none of those things? What if it's just evolution; the natural recalibration that keeps us aligned with who we're becoming?

There's real maturity in recognising when a plan needs revising. It's wise to ask not only *where* you're heading, but *why*. Does the success you once defined feel like success now? Is the pace still healthy? Does the path still belong to you, or has it started to belong to someone else's expectations?

We're living through a time when this recalibration isn't optional; it's essential. The world is shifting beneath our feet. This seismic activity can be anything from geopolitical tensions and inflationary pressures to changing workplace dynamics and the rise of AI. Budgets are tightening. Teams are smaller. Leaders are being asked to deliver the same outcomes with fewer resources. Plans made in stable conditions can collide with realities that look very different. When that happens, agility becomes a survival skill, not just a leadership buzzword.

I've lived through seismic shifts more than once. I remember when we had large-scale in-person events planned, with thousands registered, venues secured, months of preparation complete—and then Covid hit.

Overnight, every plan went out the window. We had to pivot to virtual within days and reimagine formats, technologies and team structures. It was chaotic, exhausting and, at times, overwhelming. But it also revealed something remarkable.

My team discovered skills they never knew they had. They produced live-streamed events that rivalled professional TV broadcasts. They mastered lighting, scripting and virtual audience engagement. They built resilience and creativity in real time. By the end of that year, they weren't just running digital events; they were storytelling through a new medium. The lesson that stayed with us was that you don't really know the limits of your capability until the plan collapses.

Some leaders change course after a major disruption—a restructure, a global crisis or an economic downturn. Others are prompted by a question that won't leave them alone. I once worked with a CMO who had spent months preparing for a major product launch, which became impossible to deliver due to supply chain issues. Rather than push through, she tore up the plan, re-imagined the campaign in real time and turned what could have been a disaster into a breakthrough. That's the power of revising with intent.

Revising a plan doesn't mean abandoning direction; it means adjusting it with purpose. It might mean resetting boundaries, reshaping goals or saying no to the projects that sound impressive but feel off-mission. Sometimes it means stepping sideways into a new role, a new market, or a pause that gives you the altitude to see things differently.

This kind of leadership isn't always celebrated. In cultures that idolise hustle, the courage to change direction can be mistaken for uncertainty. But those who lead with clarity know this truth: the best course corrections often happen below the radar, and are visible only through renewed focus, better energy and outcomes that last.

And yet, they are felt.

You feel them in the energy that returns after months of fatigue. In the calm that follows once the decision is made. In the steadiness that comes when your internal compass aligns again with your external world.

Revising the plan often redefines what leadership looks like. It might mean leading with more presence and less perfection and giving others space to contribute, rather than holding control. Recognising that legacy isn't built through rigid adherence, but through a pattern of choices made with integrity—especially when the winds change.

The hardest part is the in-between—that stretch of time when you know the plan needs to change, but the new direction hasn't yet emerged. You're mid-air, aware the current trajectory won't get you where you want to go, but unsure what to replace it with. Covid taught many of us that lesson.

Plans, forecasts and strategies vanished overnight, and leaders had to rebuild week by week, guided by instinct and empathy more than certainty.

I remember leading a major rebrand that was paused midstream after new leadership joined. For months, everything stalled. But in that pause, the team re-evaluated what truly mattered. What emerged was simpler, stronger and far more enduring than the original plan—proof that delay isn't always a setback and can sometimes be a refinement.

That in-between isn't a void, it's a recalibration zone. It's where reflection happens, mentors help you reframe and conversations plant the seeds of a new direction. It's where the noise fades just long enough for clarity to surface. And it's where courage lives. Because revising a plan requires faith—not in the outcome itself, but in your ability to navigate towards it.

Leadership is rarely a straight line. The most meaningful growth comes through pivots, pauses and re-imagined routes. Here's to the leaders who don't just follow a plan, but pay attention to the signals, adjust mid-flight and lead with clarity and courage. Because the goal isn't to follow the plan exactly, it's to arrive—with purpose, presence, and a deeper understanding of what truly matters.

So I invite you to consider:

- What has changed—in the market, in your world, or within you—that your plan hasn't caught up with?

- What are you holding onto out of habit, rather than conviction?

- What would happen if you allowed space for your plan to evolve?

- And who might help you see possibilities you can't yet see for yourself?

28

Cruising Without Autopilot

THERE'S A POINT in every flight when the seatbelt sign switches off, the initial turbulence has passed and the aircraft settles into cruise mode. It's smooth, steady. You exhale. It's easy to believe, in that moment, that everything is fine.

In leadership, cruising altitude can feel much the same.

The systems are running smoothly, the team is capable and the results are predictable. You know the cadence, the meetings, the milestones. The take-off adrenaline has settled. The chaos of change has calmed. You are cruising, and that can feel both earned and reassuring.

That steadiness can be a gift. But it can also be a subtle risk.

Autopilot in aviation is designed for efficiency; it prevents error through consistency. In leadership, autopilot is far more dangerous. It shows up as habitual decision-making, default answers and the slow erosion of curiosity. You're doing what works, but not always what matters. Solving for stability, but not necessarily for growth. The plane stays in the air, but the pilot stops looking out the window.

I've worked with leaders who are exceptional in crisis and inspired in the early stages of growth, but who lose spark at cruising altitude. Not because they've stopped performing, but because they can feel the air thinning. Feedback loops shrink. Curiosity fades. They know how to keep the plane in the air, but they're no longer sure why they're flying the same route. This is a different kind of leadership challenge. It's not about failure or crisis, but inertia. And it often hides behind the illusion of success. The KPIs are fine. The team looks engaged. The reports are glowing. But under the surface, drift begins. Purpose blurs. Complacency settles. And one day, a leader wakes up to find they've been flying on a route they never consciously chose.

Cruising without autopilot isn't about rejecting stability, it's about staying awake inside it. It's about continuing to *choose* how you lead rather than defaulting to what's comfortable.

So how do you do that? How do you stay alert and engaged when things feel steady?

First, you listen. Not just to the data or the dashboards, but to your internal signals and the metrics that rarely make it onto a slide deck. The heaviness you feel before a recurring meeting that once energised you. The frustration that surfaces when the work feels like repetition rather than creation. The way your patience thins in moments that used to bring joy. Those are not signs of fatigue alone; they're indicators of misalignment. They're the early turbulence before drift becomes visible.

And then, you ask yourself honestly: What am I avoiding because it might stir discomfort? What conversations am I postponing because they could change something I've grown comfortable with? What parts of my role have become about maintenance rather than meaning?

You also watch for the smaller, subtler signs. The team that once challenged your ideas now nods a little too quickly. The creative brainstorms that used to run long now end on time, every time. Feedback loops shorten, not because alignment has improved, but because curiosity has dulled. The tone of meetings shifts from energised to efficient. Those are not operational metrics; they're cultural ones. And when left unchecked, they mark the start of autopilot.

For teams, this is often when engagement begins to fade. Not dramatically, but slowly. Meetings start to sound the same. The goals feel distant. Even high performers start to coast. Without challenge or renewal, the spark that once fuelled innovation turns into routine. That's why leaders who can lead without autopilot are so valuable. They sense drift before it becomes decline. They bring curiosity into calm seasons. They find small ways to reignite energy before comfort turns into complacency.

I remember a period when my team was performing exceptionally well. Everything was running smoothly, results were strong and the feedback from across the business was glowing. But something in me felt flat. We had perfected delivery, but lost the creative pulse that had made our earlier work so distinctive. So, we decided to shake things up.

We paused our regular cadence of meetings and spent a week running what we called creative excellence sessions:

no slides, no metrics, just open problem-solving. We invited people from outside the team, asked naïve questions and revisited long-held assumptions. By the end of the week, the ideas were flowing again. Not because we'd reinvented everything, but because we'd reconnected with curiosity. That simple shift brought energy back into the work and reminded me that sometimes the leader's role is to disrupt comfort before it calcifies.

A colleague once shared how he nearly missed a major inflection point because everything looked fine. He was running a well-oiled operation; the team respected him and the numbers were steady. But one morning, he realised that he couldn't remember the last time anyone had brought him an idea he hadn't asked for. That insight hit hard. He realised he'd created a culture of delivery, not discovery. Within months, he began rotating responsibilities, creating cross-team projects and reintroducing experimentation. The business didn't just sustain, it grew—because he reawakened curiosity before complacency took root.

I attended a leadership offsite where the facilitator asked each leader to draw a flight path for their team: where did it begin, what turbulence had they weathered and where were they headed? Although many could describe their current airspace with precision, they struggled to define a shared destination. Not because they didn't care, but because they hadn't paused to reflect. They were flying well, but passively.

Leadership isn't about chasing reinvention, it's about remaining intentional. It's about knowing when your cruise control has become a comfort zone. It's knowing when to climb, when to descend, and when to pause mid-air and reconsider the route. Sometimes the answer is recalibration. Other times, it's renewal: you need a new challenge, a new collaboration or simply a new question. The courage to shift, not because you must, but because you can sense there's more ahead. And sometimes, the answer is recommitment— seeing the value in what's already working and showing up with renewed energy. Leadership isn't always about big moves. It's about conscious ones.

I once worked alongside a creative director who'd been in the same role for years. From the outside, it looked like autopilot. But every quarter, she reviewed not just performance, but energy, impact and creativity. Was she still learning? Was the team still inspired? Was she still proud of their work? If the answers dipped, she made a change and looked for a new collaboration, a different focus or a bold experiment. She didn't wait for turbulence to wake her; she stayed awake on purpose.

Cruising without autopilot doesn't mean constant movement, it means conscious motion. This can mean returning, again and again, to the questions that matter. Or choosing your flight path, even when the sky is clear. Sometimes, we mistake peace for passivity. But leadership that stays present is neither noisy nor numb. It's clear. It's curious. And it's capable of course-correcting, even mid-flight.

So I invite you to consider:

- Where in your leadership might you be gliding rather than guiding?

- What subtle signs could be hinting that comfort has become complacency?

- Where might curiosity need to be reignited?

- What would it look like to re-engage with purpose, not pressure?

29

Landing Gear

THERE'S A SUBTLE moment in every flight when the landing gear comes down. You might not see it, but you feel it; a thud beneath the cabin, a shift in sound, a slight tilt as the plane begins its descent. It's mechanical, yes, but it's also symbolic. It's the point where vision meets reality. The transition from air to earth. From momentum to arrival. From elevation to re-entry.

In leadership, we don't always notice when it's time to lower the landing gear. We're wired for ascent; the thrill of a new idea, a new role or a new market. But the real art lies not just in taking off, but in knowing when to descend. When to finish something with care and close the loop rather than chase the next horizon.

We get good at take-off; at launching visions, building momentum and pushing forward. But the art of landing, of bringing an initiative to its rightful close, is much harder. It asks for something more still: patience, empathy and attention. The ability to end well, without burning out or leaving others behind.

It asks us to slow down. To assess the conditions. To prepare the team for what's ahead. To listen for what's changed on the ground. Because landing isn't an ending; it's an act of arrival. The point where vision is translated into practice and where reflection turns into readiness.

And yet, we don't always arrive well. Sometimes we land too fast and launch the next project before we've learnt from the last. At other times, we circle endlessly, reluctant to end something that's run its course. I've seen leaders cling to outdated strategies because they fear what stopping might say about them. I've also seen teams exhausted by the pace of constant take-offs that never give them the satisfaction of a firm landing. Both patterns deplete energy—one through avoidance, the other through overdrive.

Leadership calls for real landings: intentional, grounded and human.

A strategy only matters if it takes root. A team only thrives if it knows where it stands. A leader only sustains if they know when to descend, when to close and when to finish something well. Landing gear is preparation. It's the meeting point between ambition and accountability. It's the bridge between idea and execution. It doesn't mean giving up on vision, it means honouring it enough to bring it to life properly. To shift from imagination to implementation. From inspiration to impact.

In my experience, the best leaders aren't just visionaries— they're great landers, too. They close loops. They celebrate endings. They follow through. They make transition part of the culture. I once worked with a leader who made it a rule that every major project ended with a 'touchdown meeting'. No decks, no KPIs—just stories. What worked, what we learnt, who grew. That one ritual transformed how people felt about completion. It turned closure into celebration, not fatigue.

Because the quality of a landing determines the altitude of the next take-off. Rushed landings leave friction. Unspoken endings breed confusion. Skipped celebrations erode trust. But when a leader lands with clarity and calm, something powerful happens: energy resets. Teams breathe again. Reflection creates renewal. And readiness for what's next becomes collective, not just individual.

I once led a cross-functional project that didn't go to plan. The results were mixed, and everyone felt deflated. The instinct was to move on quickly and file the bad experience away as a learning and start fresh. But instead, we paused and held what might be called a 'landing session'. Each team member shared what they were proud of, what they would do differently and what they needed to reset. It turned a potential failure into a moment of growth. The team walked out lighter, not because the outcome changed, but because we gave it a proper landing.

And that skill has never been more critical. In a world of constant motion, projects overlap and goals evolve before the ink is dry. Teams rotate, momentum replaces meaning, and we find ourselves sprinting towards the next launch without pausing to acknowledge what's just been achieved. During the Covid pandemic, I watched this play out in real time— projects that pivoted overnight, heroic efforts to adapt, but little space to debrief or decompress. By the end, people weren't short on skill, they were short on closure.

Bringing the landing gear down isn't dramatic. It's deliberate. It's a leader saying, 'We've reached a milestone. Let's land it well before we fly again.' It's a signal of awareness, maturity and respect for the rhythm of sustainable work. A leader who knows how to land well insists on a proper debrief, not as ceremony but as learning. That leader creates moments to thank the team publicly and privately. They say, 'This is the end of this phase—let's acknowledge what it took to get here before we lift off again.' That pause isn't indulgence, it's investment.

A friend and fellow leader I admire ends every quarter with her team by asking three questions: 'What are we proud of? What are we letting go of? What do we want to feel next quarter?' It's simple but powerful. Over time, it's created a culture where reflection isn't a postscript—it's part of the process. Landing has become a shared practice, not a private moment.

Leaders who know how to land also know when to call time on something that's not working. I once coached a senior leader who led a product line and had become emotionally attached to its legacy success. The numbers told a different story, but no one wanted to hear it. She chose to land it—respectfully and transparently—before it crashed. Her team later said it was the most human leadership decision they'd seen.

I had to make that call myself when I left a role that had once felt like home. I knew I'd given everything I could, but staying would have meant diminishing returns for both me and the team. Rather than disappearing into the next opportunity, I spent my final weeks ensuring my successor was set up, the team felt confident and the work was left in better shape than I found it. It wasn't easy, but it was right. Sometimes, the most powerful thing a leader can do is land well, even when it means stepping off the plane.

Leaders who land well understand that return is part of the rhythm. That no one stays at altitude forever. That ground time matters as much as airtime because it's where teams reflect, reconnect and repair. Where perspective sharpens, and future flight paths are plotted with greater wisdom.

We don't often celebrate these moments, but maybe we should. Because there's power in knowing how to arrive, not just how to aspire. In finishing well, not just starting strong. In landing with clarity, not exhaustion. Perhaps that's the true mark of enduring leadership—not how high we fly, but how skilfully we return.

So I invite you to consider:

- Where in your leadership do you need to bring the landing gear down?

- What deserves a proper landing—not because it failed, but because it's complete?

- What could closure look like for your team, in a way that re-energises rather than ends?

- And how might you design better landings for both yourself, and for those who travel with you?

30

The Creativity
We Don't
Always See

CREATIVITY HAS ALWAYS fascinated me. Not just as an output, but as a force. In many workplaces, we talk about creativity like it belongs to a department or a job title. The 'creative team'. The 'big idea'. The 'keynote-worthy concept'.

But creativity is not a department. It's a discipline that exists everywhere and in everyone.

It's in the questions we ask. The dots we connect. The way we approach a new idea or reimagine an old one. It's how we challenge ourselves to think differently; not for novelty's sake, but in pursuit of something better.

I've seen creativity in the marketer who re-engineered a process to save a team's sanity, and in the finance manager who redesigned how results were presented so that everyone finally understood the story behind the numbers. Creativity in motion is practical, human and deeply valuable.

Too often, we reduce creativity to design or messaging. If it looks good or sounds clever, we label it creative. But the most transformative creativity isn't loud, but structural. It simplifies what's tangled, rebuilds what's broken and clears the way for progress. I once worked alongside an operations lead who completely re-imagined the workflow between regional and global teams. Her redesign didn't appear on a stage, but it changed how hundreds of people worked every day. That's creativity with impact—the kind you feel, not just see.

Then there's creative courage—the kind that pushes a bold idea through all the approvals and ambiguity. Or creative intuition, which is the hunch that says, 'This matters, even if I can't explain why yet.' And creative discipline that is the less glamorous but essential ability to edit, refine and reshape. There's also creativity in constraint—in turning a limited budget, a small team or sceptical stakeholders into fuel for innovation. During a major product launch years ago, we lost half our event budget overnight. But instead of scaling back, the team leaned in. We turned what should have been a setback into a story and created a live, low-cost experience that ended up outperforming campaigns ten times its size. That's what creative constraint looks like: resourcefulness turned into resilience.

Some of the most inventive people I know aren't in creative roles. They're in operations, analytics or enablement, and constantly rethink how things work and redesign how we move through challenges. One of the best strategists I've ever worked with wouldn't call herself creative, but her mind was wired for pattern recognition. She could find clarity in chaos. She didn't need a blank canvas, she needed a tangle. And from that, she could carve out the simplest, sharpest way forward.

That's creativity.

It's also emotional. Creativity can be vulnerable. To say, 'Here's a new way we could do this,' is to risk being misunderstood or dismissed. That risk feels personal. It's exposure. Which is why psychological safety isn't just a cultural nicety, it's a creative enabler. Without trust, there's no risk. Without risk, there's no originality.

I once worked with a senior engineer who wasn't known for showmanship, but for his quiet ability to fix the things no one else could; not the systems, but the relationships. When tension built between two teams, he designed a swap week, where team members shadowed each other's work to understand their challenges firsthand. It wasn't a formal program, just an experiment born of empathy, but within a month, the friction had softened into respect. That was creativity too—the kind that rebuilds culture one small act at a time.

As leaders, we don't always realise how much power we hold in shaping the conditions for creativity. We say we want bold ideas, but do we make room for them? We say we value experimentation, but do we tolerate failure? We say we celebrate difference, but when time pressures hit, do we revert to the comfort of what's familiar? The creative culture of a team is never accidental. It's modelled.

Creativity thrives in the right mix of trust, time and tension. Trust gives people the safety to stretch. Time allows ideas to mature beyond the first draft. And tension—not conflict, but the constructive friction between diverse perspectives—helps something original emerge. I once saw this play out between a data scientist and a designer who could not have been more different. Their debates were fiery, but respectful, and the product they created was one of the smartest and most user-centred I've seen. That's creative tension at work.

The mistake many leaders make is waiting until the brainstorm to invite creativity. But creativity doesn't start with a Post-it note. It's in the clarity of a brief, the openness of a meeting or the moment you notice a junior team member hesitate before sharing an idea. It's in how we respond to something not yet fully formed, and the unpolished thought that makes you pause, not because it's perfect, but because it's honest.

And it's in how we reward people. If we only applaud the visible outcome—the pitch won, the campaign launched—we miss the invisible creativity that got us there. The idea someone quietly let go of to protect credibility. The process someone redesigned so we could move faster. The email that reset a tense dynamic and brought the team back into flow. Those unseen creative acts are incredibly important, but rarely get recognised. They are the glue that holds good work together, and the spark that makes great work possible.

In an industry that celebrates bold, visible creativity—the kind that fills stages and wins awards—I find myself drawn to the smaller sparks. The everyday acts of re-thinking, re-imagining and re-aligning that happen in meeting rooms, spreadsheets and hallway conversations.

Years ago, I met an executive assistant who quietly transformed how her organisation communicated. She noticed how long it took people to reply to complex update emails, so she started sending short, two-line summaries at the top: *Here's what's changed. Here's what's needed.* Within weeks, productivity soared. It was a simple act, but it solved a real problem. She wasn't trying to be creative; she was trying to make things clearer. And in doing so, she made the whole company work better.

These small acts are what sustain the bigger ones. These moments don't win awards, but they win trust and clarity, and strengthen teams. And they move things forward.

If we want to build truly creative teams that are capable of both brilliance and endurance, we must expand how we define creativity and who we see as creative. Because some of the greatest breakthroughs don't come from people trying to be creative, but from people simply trying to make something better. And that mindset—humble, curious and courageous—is the most creative force we have.

So I invite you to consider:

- Where is creativity already alive in your team, but perhaps unrecognised?

- What everyday acts of creativity could you bring to light?

- What conditions—of trust, time or tension—are you shaping for creativity to thrive?

- And how might you reframe your own relationship with creativity, not as something to perform, but as something you already possess?

31

Heartbreak in Transit

REMEMBER YOUR FIRST heartbreak? The kind that found you before you knew how to name it. Everything felt magnified. The world shifted shape. Songs sounded different. Mornings grew heavier. Hope flickered, faded and flickered again.

And while the ache softens over time, heartbreak never really leaves us. It just changes form.

There's heartbreak in lost love, but also in lost trust. When our belief in something or someone doesn't hold. When we pour our heart into a project, a pitch or a plan, only to watch it unravel. When we hold a vision so clearly it feels real, only to see it pass us by.

We feel it in the quiet disappointments. When a project slips away. When a role shifts. When the version of the future we were holding starts to fade.

Heartbreak isn't always cinematic. Sometimes, it's quiet, professional and private.

It arrives in boardrooms and Zoom calls. In rejection emails and 'not this time' conversations. It creeps in when a team you nurtured falls apart or a role you once loved stops loving you back. When the thing that gave you purpose no longer feels like home.

I remember a colleague sharing how, after years of building a team from scratch, a merger dissolved it overnight. 'It wasn't just losing my role,' she said. 'It was losing my people.' That kind of heartbreak can linger the longest.

I've experienced all of those. And I've come to believe that heartbreak, in all its forms, is one of the most human experiences we can have. Because to be heartbroken means you dared to care. And that's not a weakness. It's a strength. It means you showed up. You invested. You believed in something deeply enough that its absence could shake you.

In leadership, we're trained to contain, stay composed and keep moving. But sometimes the most honest thing we can do is admit: this one hurt. It might be the end of a trusted working relationship, a team restructure that leaves you grappling with guilt or an opportunity that almost came through, but didn't. We're told to brush it off. Spin it forward. Find the lesson.

But it can be hard to find the lesson. Over the last few years, I've had countless conversations with leaders across industries dealing with rounds of layoffs. These people carry the weight of telling person after person that their role no longer exists. These are people they had hired in good faith. People whose talent they saw, whose progress they championed, whose potential they believed in. There's a special kind of heartbreak in that. Because there's no tidy lesson—it just hurts. It stays with you. And it reminds you that leadership, at its core, is human work.

And while there can be learning in loss, we don't need to rush to reframe pain as progress. Sometimes, the lesson is to sit with the ache. To let it matter. To honour what it meant. Because that ache is the echo of investment. It's the evidence that we cared. That we gave a piece of ourselves to something that mattered. That we were brave enough to want something.

There's a heartbreak I remember vividly. We were so sure of the direction we were going—the strategy, the storytelling and the alignment across the business all felt right. It felt like us. We'd done the work, brought people with us, built belief. But then priorities shifted. Leadership changed. The direction was shelved. And it wasn't just the outcome that stung, it was what it represented. We'd seen what it could be. And in some quiet way, we grieved that possibility.

But here's the thing about heartbreak—it means you were in it. Not on the sidelines or half-invested, but fully there. That's a kind of creative courage I'll never apologise for.

Some of the leaders I admire most are the ones who've known heartbreak and stayed open. Who've kept their hearts in the work even after loss. Who didn't harden or retreat, but found a new way to show up. There's grace in that and a kind of quiet resilience that doesn't need to announce itself.

It's also a reminder that not all heartbreaks are final. Some things come back around. Some people grow. Some projects find new life. But whether they do or don't, we're shaped by what we learn in the gap.

One of the hardest things about heartbreak, in any form, is not knowing how long it will last.

But what I've learnt is this: It hurts for as long as it needs to. Eventually, the sharpness softens and the heaviness lifts. You begin to find beauty again, not in forgetting, but in remembering differently. You realise the hurt carved out space in you. Space for empathy. For wisdom. For a different kind of strength.

And that strength shows up in boardrooms, too.

It shows up when you lead a team through change with tenderness. When you hold space for someone else's disappointment. When you navigate tough conversations with care. When you decide to believe again in a person, an idea or yourself.

I once watched one of my team members work tirelessly towards promotion to a role she absolutely deserved. She delivered everything that could be asked of her and showed up with consistency, courage and care. But when organisational changes hit, the opportunity disappeared. Watching her survive that disappointment was its own kind of heartbreak. What stayed with me was how she responded—she took a breath, recalibrated and found a new way to grow. That quiet resilience said more about her strength than any promotion ever could.

Heartbreak teaches us that leadership isn't about being unshakeable. It's about being movable and still choosing to stand. It teaches us that success is sweeter when you've known the sting of loss. That trust, once rebuilt, is stronger. That courage isn't just about bold ideas—it's about open-heartedness.

So wherever you are, whether that's in the middle of a personal loss or a professional setback, or feeling a soft ache you haven't yet named, know that heartbreak is not the end of the story. It's part of what makes you real. Human. Brave. And maybe, just maybe, it means you're still in the arena.

So I invite you to consider:

- Where in your life or leadership have you experienced heartbreak?

- How did it change you, and what did it reveal about what truly matters to you?

- And how might you hold space for others navigating their own heartbreaks, big or small, with just a little more grace?

32

The Lounge
Where We Land

THERE'S A PARTICULAR kind of energy that surfaces when you're in the company of people who just get it. Who speak your language without explanation. Who know the weight of leading, the stretch of ambition and the quiet moments of doubt. You don't have to translate yourself. You can simply be understood.

I've come to realise that in the strongest professional communities, the ones built on curiosity, generosity and respect, that people often show up more fully as themselves than they do inside their own organisations. Without the walls of hierarchy, they relax into who they really are.

When you're not being measured by KPIs or hierarchy, something unlocks. You speak more freely. You share the idea that felt too 'out there' to bring to the Monday meeting. You admit when you're stuck. You celebrate a win without shrinking it down. You ask for help, advice or just a sounding board, and you do it without fear of judgement.

I've often had more junior people reach out to me through an industry forum that feels safe. They'll ask for advice or simply a coffee. I have a personal rule—I always say yes. It might be a thirty-minute Zoom call squeezed between meetings, but I'll make the time. Because when someone is brave enough to reach out for guidance, what they're really seeking is a moment of connection that gives them a sounding board outside their own organisation. Those conversations are rarely one way, but they remind me why I love this industry and they can offer a fresh perspective in return.

You don't need to posture or protect. Because you're not performing—you're participating. In the right professional community, ambition doesn't feel threatening. Vulnerability doesn't feel risky. And asking big questions—about leadership, impact, career, identity—isn't seen as indulgent, but essential.

For many years, I've invested in the broader industry. That investment has been returned in more ways than I can count. It's given me a network of people I can call or message at midnight from another time zone, who might be battling through the same chaos that I am. Those conversations help me see things differently, not because we always agree, but because we share a foundation of trust. When you're speaking with people who share your values, both professional and creative, you absorb their perspective differently. You listen more carefully. You learn faster. And you're reminded that leadership doesn't have to be lonely.

I've experienced this most powerfully through industry associations, creative festivals, and even the informal circles that form after long days of discussion. Once, during a festival, I joined a spontaneous late-night conversation where several senior leaders began brainstorming creative solutions to a big industry challenge. None of them would have been comfortable having that discussion back in their own companies. But in that environment—surrounded by peers *who got it*—they spoke freely. You could see ideas forming, talk tracks sharpening and confidence returning. Those are the kinds of moments that send you back to your day job feeling energised and renewed.

It's in these spaces that I've witnessed (and offered) some of the most honest conversations about career ceilings, burnout, imposter syndrome and what it really takes to lead in this industry. And I've noticed that the more I allow myself to be seen, the more others do the same. There's a strength in that kind of mutual unveiling, when we can drop the polished LinkedIn version of ourselves and be the real one—the version that is still learning, still doubting, still dreaming.

That's where the magic lives.

Some of us are lucky to work in environments that foster deep trust and psychological safety. But even the best workplaces come with a context—politics, pressure, power structures—that can limit how much of ourselves we're willing or able to reveal. It's not always intentional. Sometimes it's just the pace and the focus on output. The need to be 'on' all the time. And in those settings, it can feel easier to keep certain things hidden: ambitions we fear might be misunderstood, feedback we haven't processed yet, ideas we haven't found the words for.

That's why external communities matter so much. They create a parallel space where the stakes feel lower, but the connection runs deeper. They give you permission to think out loud. To be in beta. To be bold, or unsure, or both.

For leaders, this external perspective is vital. It stops us from becoming encultured—so shaped by one company's way of thinking that we stop seeing other possibilities. Some of the best ideas I've brought back to my team began as small, off-the-record conversations in communities like these.

If you've ever walked into a room and exhaled—really exhaled—because you knew you didn't have to explain why you care so much, or why you push so hard, or why you sometimes question your next move, then you know what I'm talking about.

That's the power of finding your people.

It's not just about networking or brand building. It's about being part of something that sees you beyond your title. It's about surrounding yourself with people who want to see you thrive, and who'll challenge you, cheer you on and call you forward when needed. Sometimes those people are mentors. Sometimes they're peers. Sometimes they're ten years behind you, but they remind you what drive and optimism look like in their purest form.

And sometimes, you're that person for someone else.

One of the most powerful things I've learnt is that community isn't just about connection. It's about courage. It takes courage to share what you really want. To name the fear. To say, 'I'm not sure,' or 'I've never done this before,' or even 'I want more.' But when you say it in the company of people who hold that space with care, courage becomes contagious. And from there, everything opens. The ideas get bigger. The goals get bolder. The setbacks feel less isolating. The leadership feels more human.

Because you're not doing it alone.

So I invite you to consider:

- Do you have a professional community where you can be honest about what you're wrestling with, not just what you've achieved?

- When was the last time you sought an external perspective—from someone outside your company's culture who could help you see your challenges differently?

- And who might be waiting for you to start that conversation to be the one who says, 'Me too,' and opens the door?

33

Brand as a Belief System

WHEN I THINK about the brands I'm most drawn to, it's never just because of what they sell. It's because of what they stand for. They believe in something. Not just in their product. Not just in their market. But in an idea larger than themselves. It's something you can feel in their work, even if they never say it out loud.

It might sound idealistic, but I've come to see it as one of the most strategic assets a brand can have—belief, a point of view. A sense of what matters, and the courage to stand by it when it counts.

The strongest brands don't just sell solutions, they articulate a worldview. They reflect something back to us about how we want to operate, who we want to be and where we believe the world is heading.

That kind of clarity is magnetic.

It shows up in subtle ways—in the tone of a campaign or the language on a product page. It's in the choices a company makes when no one's watching. It's not performative or loud—it's embedded. It's the reason behind the strategy and the value behind the voice.

And this isn't just about brand building. It's about leadership.

I worked with a brand that chose to delay a major campaign launch because their customers were facing an unexpected crisis. They redirected the entire media budget to supporting relief efforts. It wasn't performative, and there was no fanfare. It simply aligned with what they believed. That single act built more trust than any campaign could have.

In my own journey, I've come to believe that the most trusted leaders operate the same way. The ones we follow, even when things are uncertain, aren't always the ones with the biggest titles or the most polished credentials. They're the ones who are consistent. The ones who know what they value and live it with clarity. They speak from alignment, not just experience.

I once worked for a leader who made a difficult call to turn down a lucrative deal because it didn't align with the company's values. It wasn't a popular decision and it cost us short-term growth, but it strengthened trust—both internally and externally. People remembered that decision years later, not because of what it cost, but because of what it proved.

This is where brand and leadership intersect.

Because when you lead a brand or a team, you're not just delivering outcomes. You're shaping identity.

You're deciding what gets amplified. What gets rewarded. What gets protected. And what gets left behind. Leadership, at its core, is an act of branding. You're creating belief systems in real time.

Across every category and business model I've worked in, this remains true. When people believe in what a brand stands for, they're far more likely to engage, advocate and stay loyal—even when the road gets bumpy. Even when the product isn't perfect. Belief creates resilience.

And belief also gives brands permission to grow. The ones with a clear centre can stretch in new directions without losing their sense of self. They can evolve offerings, enter new markets or change their tone and still feel familiar. That's because belief acts like gravity. It holds everything together, even in motion.

But belief doesn't happen by accident. It's not something we find; it's something we choose. And it takes discipline to maintain it. Sometimes this means saying no to a quick win. Sometimes it means backing an idea that no one else sees. Often, it means listening deeply to customers, to employees, and to your own inner compass to make sure what you're building still aligns with what you believe.

During a difficult year, I watched a team resist the temptation to copy a competitor's trending tactic. Instead, they stayed anchored in their own story and refined how they told it. The results didn't come instantly, but when they did, they were stronger and more sustainable because they came from alignment, not imitation.

There's a temptation in business to follow the crowd and chase what's trending. To dilute the message in the name of growth. But the brands that lead—truly lead—are the ones with the courage to stay close to their convictions. They know who they are. And they're willing to show it. This is also a responsibility. Because belief, when done well, cascades.

A brand that stands for something people want to believe in tends to attract those who share that conviction. When a company publicly commits to sustainability, equity or innovation and follows through, it signals more than purpose. It becomes a magnet for like-minded customers, employees and partners. Employees who want to build something meaningful. Partners who want to co-create. Customers who want to stay. That kind of alignment is hard to replicate and even harder to fake.

In many ways, belief becomes culture. Not just internally, but externally, too. It informs tone, decisions and reputation. And as leaders, we are often the stewards of that culture, whether we realise it or not.

So the question isn't just what your brand offers. It's what it believes and whether that belief is being shown clearly— not just in the big campaigns, but in the small, consistent moments. In how you lead. In how your team shows up. In what you choose to do when no one is clapping.

That's the kind of brand people want to follow. And that's the kind of leader people trust.

So I invite you to consider:

- What does your brand or your leadership stand for beyond products, profit or performance?

- How consistently does that belief show up in your decisions, your culture and your communication?

- Where might that belief be tested next, and what would it look like to hold steady when it is?

34

Cabin
Pressure

EADERSHIP OFTEN LOOKS calm from the outside. We see the confident speaker, the composed decision-maker, the one who holds steady in moments of tension. And yet, anyone who has sat in the cockpit of modern leadership knows: there is pressure. Not always visible. Not always acknowledged. But undeniably there.

We don't talk about cabin pressure enough.

I don't mean the corporate kind—the slide decks and shareholder updates—but the internal kind. The slow build-up of expectations, responsibility and emotional labour that leaders often carry silently. The sense of needing to show up strong, especially when others are looking to you for direction, energy or reassurance.

Like the pressurised cabin of a plane, leadership environments can create a subtle force that wears on you over time. You're breathing. You're functioning. But it takes more effort than you realise. Until suddenly, something small hits differently. The offhand comment. The missed deadline. The eighth meeting in a row with no pause. And you feel it: the pressure.

I remember an intense period of event execution when everything looked great—execution flawless, targets met, team energised—but I was running on fumes. I didn't realise it until a friend asked a simple question, 'When did you last have time to feel proud rather than just relieved?' It stopped me cold. That's when I recognised how invisible pressure can become when you normalise it.

Sometimes it arrives as tension in your shoulders. Other times as shortness of breath. A dip in motivation or a spike in reactivity. It can manifest in over-functioning or withdrawal. In pushing harder or shutting down. And often, no one sees it coming. Because that's the thing about cabin pressure. From the outside, everything seems fine.

A senior leader told me that during the pandemic, she became an expert at appearing calm while juggling remote schooling, budget cuts and a level of burnout she couldn't yet name. 'I smiled through screens,' she said, 'but every Friday I closed my laptop and sat in silence for an hour, just trying to feel like myself again.' That's how invisible pressure hides—in professionalism that looks composed, but is powered by depletion.

Over the years, I've seen this in many of the most effective, well-loved leaders I know. The ones who carry their teams through restructures, campaigns, crises and wins. The ones who hold space for others but rarely find room for themselves. The ones who are told they're resilient but inside are running on a kind of emotional autopilot just to make it through the week.

These are not signs of weakness. They are signs of containment and absorbing more than is visible, and doing it in the service of others. But even the strongest cabins need decompression. Even the most seasoned flyers need oxygen.

A client once described how her 'decompression' moment came after a year of constant change. Every Friday, she booked thirty minutes alone in an empty meeting room— not to think, but to stop thinking. She said it was the only time she could breathe without an agenda. That small ritual became her release valve, and it reminded me how essential intentional pauses can be.

And here's the complexity: leadership is often structured around pressure. KPIs. Deadlines. Quarterly expectations. The pace rarely lets up, and yet the expectation is that leaders remain steady. The unspoken belief is that pressure makes diamonds.

But it can also crack the frame.

In the current economic climate, with tighter budgets and workforce reductions across industries, I've seen many leaders question whether the pace and pressure they're upholding can truly last. It's no longer just about resilience; it's about redesign and finding ways to lead that protect the human capacity required to deliver.

And the most dangerous kind of cabin pressure? The kind that builds slowly. Incrementally. The pressure of performing while parenting. Of delivering results while navigating personal health challenges. Of leading teams through layoffs while privately wondering what comes next. The type of pressure that accumulates not through one major event, but through the constancy of being the one who holds it all.

In my own leadership journey, I've come to learn that recognising pressure isn't a liability, but a skill. Because when you can name it, you can manage it. You can create vents. That vent can be a trusted peer, a walk around the block or a clear boundary around your calendar. Sometimes it's a good night's sleep, or a hard conversation, or simply saying, 'Not today.' Other times, it's giving yourself permission to not have the answer. To say, 'I don't know yet.' Or to admit, 'This is a lot right now.'

I've noticed that when I do this openly, even just once in a team meeting, it changes the air in the room. People breathe easier when they see that it's safe to say they're under pressure too. Leaders are often taught to perform certainty. But the most grounded ones I know are fluent in honesty. Not the kind that offloads everything, but the kind that creates room for real connection. The kind that builds trust because it acknowledges reality.

We are not meant to be in pressurised cabins indefinitely. No one can sustain that. And the truth is, people feel more held by a leader who is human than one who is invincible. This doesn't mean falling apart in front of your team. It means not pretending you're made of steel. It means naming the moment, inviting support and modelling what it looks like to lead with care—for others and for yourself. Because just like altitude, pressure fluctuates. Sometimes it's a high-stakes presentation. Other times, it's the slow fatigue of a heavy season. Leadership that endures isn't about avoiding pressure, it's about learning when and how to release it.

This might mean declining a speaking opportunity to make rest a priority. It might mean finally having that conversation you've been avoiding. It might mean booking a day off when it's inconvenient, but essential.

It might mean asking your own leader for support, even when you're used to being the one that others come to.

We often talk about leadership in terms of grit, endurance and strength. And yes, those qualities matter. But I believe there's a softer strength in recognising when the cabin pressure is too high. In knowing that self-regulation is not self-indulgence, but a leadership skill.

If the cost of your steadiness is your wellbeing, the system is off. There is space here to lead differently. With oxygen. With honesty. With the kind of grace that says, 'I am not limitless, and that is not a flaw.' Leadership is not just about guiding others through turbulence. It's also about maintaining your own capacity to breathe. To think clearly. To lead well, not just long.

So I invite you to consider:

- Where is the pressure building for you?
- What are your warning signs when the cabin gets tight?
- What release valve might you need to install this season?

35

The Rational Case for Emotion

THERE'S A PARTICULAR kind of decision that surfaces often in leadership. One that doesn't immediately make sense on paper. The business case isn't air-tight. The data is directional at best. There's no clear benchmark to follow. And yet, something about it feels right.

These are the moments that challenge our relationship with logic. Because even when the facts are incomplete, our instinct sometimes leads the way. And when those choices play out successfully, we often find ourselves working backwards, packaging them neatly in rationale, strategy and post-event analysis.

It's not deception, but something much more human. It's what leaders do when we rationalise the irrational.

Because we are not purely rational beings—we are rationalising beings.

In leadership, especially in marketing, the ability to recognise that, to use it well and to still lead with clarity and conviction, is a quiet but critical strength. There's a prevailing idea in business that logic is the highest currency. That if we just build the right case, show the right numbers and organise the right evidence, the best decisions will reveal themselves. But the fact is, some of our most meaningful choices are felt before they're proved.

A CMO once stood in front of her board defending a bold creative concept that every data point advised against. She said simply, 'This is the story our customers need right now—not the one our spreadsheets want.' It wasn't sentiment, it was conviction. Months later, the campaign delivered record engagement, but the real impact was internal. It shifted how the business thought about risk—from something to be avoided to something that could reveal truth.

That's where emotion comes in. Not as an opposing force to logic, but as a complement to it. Not as a threat to performance, but as a catalyst for it. Emotion is not a weakness in leadership. It's a signal. A strategy. A source of momentum.

In marketing, we talk a lot about connection, but connection isn't forged through numbers alone. It's built through resonance and through storytelling. Through the ability to reach someone in a way they remember, not just understand.

I once led a creative approach that didn't test well in pre-launch research. The numbers suggested we pull back. But there was something undeniably human in the work; it reflected a truth our audience felt but rarely said out loud. We trusted that instinct, launched it anyway, and it went on to become one of the most effective campaigns of the year. The data caught up later.

The most enduring campaigns are rarely the most efficient. They're the ones that feel true. That reflect a deeper human insight. That know how to stir something just enough to leave a mark. Those moments don't usually emerge from spreadsheets. They emerge from empathy.

The same is true inside a business. Leaders don't inspire with perfect information; they inspire with presence and intuition. With the ability to sense what's needed and act, even when it's difficult to explain in bullet points. One leader I deeply respect described this as 'reading the emotional current of the room.' She said, 'Logic tells me what's happening. Emotion tells me why.' That ability to hear what isn't being said is often what turns a good decision into a great one.

This doesn't mean ignoring data. Evidence still matters. Discipline still matters. But the reality is, the data rarely tells us what to do. It tells us what is. Leadership is what happens in the space between that and what could be.

Emotion is often seen as risky. In boardrooms, we default to language that sounds rational. We strip out the personal, the intuitive and the uncertain, and we call it focus. Or alignment. But often, it's just fear—fear that emotion will make us seem unprepared or unprofessional.

But emotion, when guided by experience and values, is one of the most powerful tools a leader can use. It's what allows us to choose clarity over consensus, to sense when something is off before it's visible, and to speak to a customer, a colleague or an audience in a way that truly sticks.

It's not about sentimentality. It's about making room for meaning.

Many of the most powerful decisions in leadership are not purely logical. They're layered. They draw on pattern recognition, memory, personal context and intuition. They rely on our ability to read a room, to listen between the lines and to pick up on the things that aren't on the slide. It's afterwards that we often do the tidy-up work. We find the metrics and build the case. We explain it in terms the business can absorb.

That's not a flaw. That's fluency.

Understanding this duality, of heart and head, is essential to building trust. Because people follow leaders who are clear, but also human. Who know when to move, even when certainty hasn't caught up yet.

In the realm of brand building, the same principle applies. People don't just buy based on logic; they buy based on how something makes them feel. They want to align with a brand that reflects how they see the world, or how they want to see it.

This is why emotional intelligence in leadership is not just a personal asset, it's a commercial one. It influences how decisions are made, how teams are built and how brands are experienced. So rather than framing emotion as a liability we must manage, what if we treated it as a leadership muscle? One we can train, stretch and use with intention. Because when logic reaches its limits, it's emotion that moves us. And sometimes, that movement is exactly what's needed.

So I invite you to consider:

- Where in your leadership are you over-indexing on logic at the expense of connection?

- What instinct or emotion have you rationalised instead of trusting?

- How might you use emotion more intentionally—not as the opposite of data, but as the signal that gives it meaning?

- And what could become possible if you trusted what you feel as much as what you know?

36

The Familiar
Things

N A WORLD that constantly celebrates the new—the next innovation, the fresh idea, the breakthrough moment— I've come to appreciate the quiet, restorative power of the familiar.

There's science behind why so many of us, when exhausted or overwhelmed, reach for the familiar. It's not laziness or nostalgia; it's regulation. Rewatching a show you've seen a dozen times, hearing the opening notes of a favourite song or drinking coffee from the same chipped mug every morning calms the nervous system by reminding the brain: *we're safe here.*

These are not acts of nostalgia. They are rituals of restoration.

In times of stress or burnout, or when life feels heavy, our instinct is often to reinvent; to reset, to push forward, to force change. But sometimes, the most grounding thing isn't a breakthrough, but a return. A return to something that reminds us of who we are when everything else feels unsteady. The part of us that exists underneath the striving. The rhythm that does not need noise to feel important. There is a kind of calm that only familiarity brings.

Think of the movie you know line by line, the book with dog-eared pages, the person who knew you long before titles or timelines mattered. These small comforts might seem trivial, but they anchor us when the world feels unstable. They pull us back from the edge of performance and reconnect us with the parts of ourselves that do not need to be impressive, only present.

I have often found that in my most demanding moments, it's not silence I need. It is return.

Return to rhythm. To memory. To what is already known and loved. There's comfort in predictability when everything else feels unpredictable. It doesn't fix the chaos, but it reminds us that not everything has to be solved. Some things can simply be held. Familiarity is not stagnation. It is a form of safety. Of softness. It gives us permission to rest in what does not demand something new from us.

In leadership, we rarely talk about this. We are encouraged to be visionaries, to chase innovation, to stretch and scale and boldly reimagine. Yes, there is value in that. But it is equally important to remember what holds us steady while we stretch. Endurance comes from a rhythm you can return to. When leaders keep a few stable rituals, ambition sustains instead of frays.

What steadies us is not always something profound. Sometimes, it's a morning ritual. A favourite song on repeat. A story we have heard a hundred times, but still smile through.

These are not distractions from the work. They are what keep us human enough to do it well.

Some of the most effective leaders I know have rituals that seem ordinary, but are deeply protective. A walk around the same neighbourhood block. A daily journal entry. A phone call every Friday with someone who knew them long before leadership became part of their job description. These small, familiar things help us metabolise the complexity we carry. They do not erase the stress, but they soften it. They regulate us. They remind us that beneath the decisions, the decks and the deliverables, we are still people.

And people need more than progress.

We need presence.

I have started to pay attention to my own patterns, noticing when I feel grounded and what helps me get there. It's often not the big things, but the familiar things. The same playlist I have been curating for over a decade. The handwritten note I keep in my drawer from someone I admire. The way I make coffee; slow, before the noise starts. Sometimes before a meeting I know will be intense, I take a few quiet minutes in the car. I put on that same playlist and sing along softly. By the time I walk in, my pulse has slowed and my mind feels clearer. It's a small act, but it brings me back to myself before I step back into the pace.

There is something about these rituals that reminds me I am still me. Even when the work is stretching. Even when life feels like too much. They anchor me in something that does not need proving and return me to myself. And when I return to myself, I can return to others more fully, too.

In teams, in families, in communities, this matters. Because when leaders are disconnected from their own centre, it ripples. It shows up as impatience. As reactivity. As overwhelm disguised as urgency. But when we are connected to ourselves, even in small ways, we make different choices. We hold space more generously. We lead with more grace. We listen more deeply.

A C-Suite leader I know runs the same three-kilometre loop before any major business review; she says it 'resets her inner noise'. Her board presentations are sharper, but more importantly, her presence is calmer, and the room follows.

Familiarity creates a foundation for that kind of leadership. It does not make the chaos disappear, but it helps us stay upright within it. That's why I no longer dismiss these small practices. They are not indulgent—they are essential. Because it is hard to lead others well when you are unmoored. When everything around you feels new, uncertain or relentlessly changing, the familiar can be a quiet act of resistance.

Sometimes, introducing familiarity can be as simple as how a meeting begins. In one of my teams, we started every weekly catch-up with the same two questions. It wasn't the questions themselves that mattered—it was the predictability. People knew what to expect, so they didn't feel caught off guard, even on stressful days. Over time, that small ritual became a rhythm that steadied everyone before the work began.

In many ways, that's what the familiar offers us—a soft return. It reminds us that steadiness often comes from repetition, not reinvention. That we are allowed to be people first. We do not always need to leap forward. Sometimes, we just need to return. Return to what feels like exhaling. Return to the rhythms that help us breathe again.

Leadership is not just about charting new paths, it's about remembering the ones that held us when we were lost. It's about trusting that the familiar does not make you less ambitious, less bold or less ready. It makes you steady. And that steadiness is what allows you to keep going.

So if you are tired, or overwhelmed, or caught in the churn of change, know this. You do not always need a new tool, a new mindset or a dramatic shift. Sometimes you just need a small return. To the things that are already yours. To the places that ask nothing of you. To the people who see you clearly. To the rituals that remind you who you are.

These are the familiar things. And they are not small at all.

So I invite you to consider:

- When life feels uncertain, what familiar rhythms bring you back to yourself?

- What rituals, people or places remind you that you are safe and whole?

- And how might you build more space for familiarity; not as comfort alone, but as a quiet form of strength?

Where to Now?
Still in the In–Between?

T HE IN-BETWEEN IS not a metaphor.

It is literal; the moments between what's next and what's now. The pause between meetings. The taxi ride after a long day. The time on a flight when the Wi-Fi won't connect and you can't do anything except think. These are the spaces where reflection finds you, not because you planned it, but because the pace of life forces you to stop. That is where real leadership often re-centres itself.

This book was written in those in-between spaces. Not as a manual or a how-to guide, but as an honest reflection of how leadership really feels in moments of tension and uncertainty, and in the times when we keep going even without all the answers.

It started mid-flight—somewhere between boarding passes and baggage claims. I stopped filling the time with distractions and started craving stillness; not to switch off, but to tune in. I began jotting down thoughts at altitude; small reflections typed into my phone while the world moved below.

I called it *Between Flights* because that's exactly when and where it began. I expected very little, but what came back was unforgettable: the encouragement, the messages from people who felt seen in these reflections, the stories of leadership and growth shared back with me. I will never forget those responses and will always be deeply grateful for them.

Over time, it became more than a writing practice. It became a record of the moments in leadership that don't always make headlines, but shape how we show up. Each reflection began as one flight, one thought, one attempt to make sense of what mattered most at that time.

Writing these chapters gave me perspective, clarity and self-confidence. They became a reminder that progress doesn't always come from moving faster, but from paying attention. If even one page has helped you feel seen, steadied or more aligned in how you lead, then I am deeply grateful.

Across these reflections, we have explored what leadership really looks like behind the scenes: the juggle between ambition and care, the courage to make creative choices, the pressure of performance and the pauses that restore us. We've talked about confidence, patience, legacy and the power of saying no. Together, these chapters form a mosaic of what modern leadership feels like: messy, human and full of heart. As we move forward, it isn't about becoming someone new; it's about becoming more grounded in who we already are. Leadership evolves as we do.

The in-between moments always find us—sometimes in times of uncertainty, sometimes in moments of renewal. Each one gives us a chance to realign and to notice what matters most and how we want to show up next. These pauses are rarely comfortable, but they often teach us more than momentum ever could.

Some of the most important decisions of my career weren't made in moments of celebration or crisis. They were made in the middle: on long flights, in quiet car rides, or during late nights when reflection finally caught up. The in-between teaches patience. It slows us down when everything else demands speed and reminds us that growth needs space, not urgency.

There have been seasons when I wasn't who I had been, but not yet who I was becoming. When leadership meant listening instead of leading. When confidence felt uncertain, but something more true was forming. I used to see those pauses as lost time. Now I see them as the ground where the next version of me was taking shape.

We don't talk much about these phases because they aren't polished or public. They don't make for highlight reels. But they matter, because they're where we test our values, reset boundaries and reconnect with why we lead.

So where to from here?

I hope you'll return to this book on a future flight, or share a chapter with a colleague who's carrying more than they let on. I hope you'll start noticing your own in-between moments more clearly and give them the attention they deserve.

I'm so grateful that you've spent time with these words. Thank you for reading, for reflecting, and for bringing your own experiences into this conversation. The gate is open now, and wherever you go next is yours to choose. Take what resonates and leave what doesn't. I wish you every success, happiness and joy as you move forward—wherever your next chapter takes you.

Reflections
in Practice

OFTEN, REFLECTION BEGINS when something interrupts our rhythm: a conversation, a moment of uncertainty, a pause we didn't plan. But we don't have to wait for those moments to find perspective. We can choose them.

These exercises are an invitation to do just that; to create those small moments of pause *between flights*, to take stock of where you are, how you're leading and what might need recalibration. None of them take long to complete, but each one can offer powerful food for thought; gentle prompts that help you return to work, and to yourself, with more intention.

The first reflection begins where all meaningful leadership does—with gratitude. Gratitude for the people, lessons and moments that have shaped us, and for the legacy we're building through the way we show up every day. It's a theme that threads through much of this work, because gratitude grounds clarity and reminds us of what truly matters before we look forward to what's next.

In leadership, reflection is not a luxury, it's a practice. It strengthens awareness, deepens empathy and sharpens decision-making. These simple frameworks can help you uncover what fuels you, where your energy is going, and which relationships need more care or clarity. Over time, they become less of an exercise and more of a rhythm; a way to stay aligned even when the pace around you accelerates.

They explore the different dimensions of modern leadership: energy and balance, relationships and influence, boundaries and creativity, purpose and growth. Together, they form a toolkit for reflection, which is simple in structure but designed to meet you wherever you are in your journey.

So wherever you find yourself—in motion, in pause or somewhere in between—let these reflections meet you there. Use them to realign, to rediscover, and to remind yourself that clarity is often waiting just beneath the surface.

Included Reflections:

1   **The Grateful Legacy:** Mapping gratitude as the foundation of the legacy you build through your work and leadership.

2   **Rebalancing the Energy Equation**: Re-aligning how you give and receive energy across life and leadership.

3   **The Personal Boardroom:** Identifying the people who ground, challenge and champion your growth.

4   **The Relationship Alignment Map:** Assessing and strengthening the relationships that shape how effectively you lead.

5   **The Yes Inventory:** Re-examining what you've agreed to and whether it still aligns with your purpose.

6   **The Creativity Integrity Scan:** Reconnecting your creative decisions to your values and courage.

7   **The Career Compass Check:** Looking back to see how your leadership story has evolved and where it's ready to go next.

8   **The Alignment Audit:** Reviewing where your actions, values and priorities are in sync—and where they've drifted.

9   **The Decision Debrief:** Reflecting on recent decisions to extract lessons, patterns and future clarity.

10 **The Trust Ledger:** Evaluating where trust flows freely in your work and where it might need rebuilding.

11 **The Pause Plan:** Designing intentional moments of stillness to restore clarity and creative energy.

12 **The Feedback Mirror:** Using feedback as a lens for growth, self-awareness and more empathetic leadership.

Reflection Exercise
The Grateful Legacy

LEGACY IS NOT built at the end of our journey, it's created in the way we show up along the way. It lives in our choices, our gratitude and the small ways we shape the experiences of others. This reflection is about tracing the line between what we've received, what we've given and what remains after we've moved on. Gratitude helps us see that line clearly and it reminds us that every person, moment and lesson leaves an imprint.

Here's how it works:

1   Draw two columns on a page. Label one *What I've been given* and the other *What I'm giving forward*.

This is your map—a visual of how gratitude becomes legacy.

2   Begin with what you've been given. Think of the people, opportunities and defining moments that have shaped you—the mentors who believed in you, the colleagues who challenged you, the projects that stretched your limits, the setbacks that taught you resilience. Write them down, one by one, and next to each, note what you're grateful for.

For example:

'For teaching me patience.'
'For reminding me that kindness can be powerful.'
'For showing me what courage looks like in practice.'

3   Now turn to what you're giving forward. Look across the page and reflect on how you pass those lessons on—in how you lead, support, or inspire others.

For example:

Maybe you mentor because someone once mentored you.

Maybe you lead with empathy because you remember what it felt like to be unseen.

Maybe you build creative cultures because someone once gave you space to try.

4   Connect the dots. Draw lines between the lessons you've received and the ways you're expressing them now.

You'll start to see patterns—a living map of gratitude in action.

5   Reflect on what remains. If you were to leave your role tomorrow, what would you hope people remember?

A sense of calm in the chaos? A culture of creativity? The way you made them feel capable and seen?

Write one or two sentences that capture that intention—not as a final legacy, but as a daily practice of gratitude in motion.

For example:

'I want my work to remind people that kindness and excellence can co-exist.'

'I hope the spaces I build make others feel brave enough to create.'

'I want to be remembered not for the pace I kept, but for the care I gave.'

When we lead with gratitude, our legacy begins to write itself— quietly and consistently through the lives we touch. Gratitude anchors us in meaning and ensures that what we build is not only successful, but significant.

Reflection Exercise
Rebalancing the Energy Equation

SOMETIMES THE LIFT comes back once we stop to notice what's fuelling us and what's quietly draining us.

When I'm stretched or feeling off balance, this is a simple exercise I turn to. It helps me name what's really going on beneath the busyness: where I'm pouring too much, where I'm holding back and what might need a small shift. It's not perfect, but it helps bring things back into focus. Maybe it will for you too.

Here's how it works:

1   Draw a circle and divide it into six segments.

2   Label each one with a part of your life that matters to you right now.

- Work (or split into multiple categories like leadership, projects, team)
- Family
- Health
- Personal growth
- Creativity
- Relationships or friendships
- Rest or downtime
- Anything else that feels important

3   For each one, give yourself two scores (from 1 to 10):

- One for how much energy you're putting in
- One for how much energy you're getting back

4   Now pause and take a look.

- Are there segments where you're consistently giving more than you're receiving?
- Or areas you've unintentionally neglected, even though they matter to you?

5   Choose one segment that feels off balance.

- Write down one small shift—a boundary, a commitment, or a gentle reframe—that could help bring you closer to alignment.

This isn't about perfection or fixing everything overnight. It's about noticing where you are, and what might need a little more care, because when your energy is aligned with your values, the lift comes more naturally.

Reflection Exercise
The Personal Boardroom

IF LEADERSHIP IS about who we bring with us, this exercise helps
you name the people who anchor, challenge and elevate you.

Here's how it works:

1 Draw a table with six seats—your personal boardroom.

2 Think about who currently sits in those seats in your life:

   • The Truth Teller (the one who calls it as it is)
   • The Encourager (who reminds you what's possible)
   • The Connector (who opens doors)
   • The Challenger (who sharpens your thinking)
   • The Grounder (who helps you stay balanced)
   • The Mirror (who reflects your best self back to you)

3 Write the names of people who fill those roles, or leave a
   seat open if no one fits yet.

4 Reflect on:

   • Who needs to be called in closer?
   • Who might you be missing right now?
   • How can you be that person for someone else?

This is a practical way to bring more intention to your support
network and to ensure your leadership stays grounded in connection, not just capability.

Reflection Exercise
The Relationship Alignment Map

NO LEADER SUCCEEDS alone. Behind every milestone, there are relationships that make it possible—the manager who opens doors, the peer who challenges your thinking, the stakeholder who trusts your judgement. And sometimes, the distance between how we *think* those relationships are going and how others *feel* they're going can define our effectiveness. This exercise helps you take stock of the connections that matter most to your work, and to see where a little recalibration might create more trust, collaboration or momentum.

Here's how it works:

1 List your key relationships. Think about the people who influence your ability to deliver in your role and how you're perceived in doing it.

   - Your manager
   - Your team
   - Peers and cross-functional partners
   - Key stakeholders or sponsors
   - Anyone whose confidence and collaboration directly impact your success

2 Rate the importance. Next to each person or group, rate from 1 to 10 how important that relationship is to your success—both in achieving outcomes and in being seen as effective.

3   Step into their shoes. Now, put yourself in their position and ask, 'If they were rating our relationship, what score might they give it?'

Be honest. Think about recent interactions, communication flow, trust, responsiveness and mutual understanding.

4   Spot the gaps. Compare the two scores.

- Where is the difference more than two or three points?

- What might be causing that gap—unmet expectations, communication habits, or time since your last meaningful interaction?

- What could you do to strengthen the connection?

5   Choose one relationship to nurture. Small, consistent actions often make the biggest difference—a check-in, a word of appreciation, an invitation to collaborate.

This reflection isn't about people-pleasing, it's about perspective. It helps you see your network as a living system that needs attention and alignment to thrive. Because when your relationships are strong, your leadership naturally follows.

Reflection Exercise
The Yes Inventory

THIS REFLECTION IS designed to help you look honestly at where your 'yes' is going, and what that means for your time, focus and energy.

Here's how it works:

1 Take a fresh page and draw three columns:

   - *Yes I must*
   - *Yes I should reconsider*
   - *Yes I can release*

2 Under *Yes I must*, list the commitments that align strongly with your purpose, values or essential responsibilities. These are the things that truly matter.

3 Under *Yes I should reconsider*, list the things you've taken on that feel more habitual or obligation-based than intentional. Ask: 'If I said no to this, what would really happen?'

4 Under *Yes I can release*, write the things that no longer serve you, your growth or your wellbeing. They might have once fit your goals but don't any more.

Now step back and look at the page.

- How many of the ones you marked as 'yes' feel energising versus draining?

- Where could a single 'no' create more space for what matters most?

- What boundaries or conversations might need to follow this reflection?

This isn't about doing less for the sake of it. It's about making space for meaning, not just momentum.

Reflection Exercise
The Creativity Integrity Scan

COURAGE IN CREATIVITY often begins with clarity. This exercise helps you and your team reflect on where you're playing it too safe and where there's space to be braver.

Here's how it works:

1   Draw three columns and label them:

  - *Ideas we're proud of*
  - *Ideas we played safe on*
  - *Ideas we wish we'd fought harder for*

2   Under each column, write specific examples from the past year.

3   For each 'safe' or 'wish we'd fought harder' example, ask:

  - What stopped us?
  - What did we fear we'd lose?
  - What might have happened if we'd gone bolder?

4   Discuss or reflect on patterns. Are you noticing a culture of caution or confidence?

Then, pick one small area where you can stretch next time— a pilot, a pitch or a project—and decide in advance what creative courage would look like there.

Reflection Exercise
The Career Compass Check

THE AIM OF this reflection is to recalibrate. To check that the direction you're flying in still aligns with who you're becoming.

Here's how it works:

1   Write down your top three priorities for the next six months. These can be personal, professional or a mix of both.

2   Next, write three questions:

  - What am I learning right now?
  - Where am I growing?
  - What am I tolerating that no longer fits?

3   Circle anything that feels misaligned or heavy.

4   For each one, ask, 'What would one small adjustment look like?'

Sometimes we don't need a complete overhaul, just a gentle course correction. This reflection helps you find it.

Reflection Exercise
The Alignment Audit

THERE ARE TIMES in leadership when we feel slightly off course without knowing why. Often, it's not because we've lost direction, but because our actions have drifted a few degrees from our values. This reflection helps you pause, recalibrate, and ensure that what you're doing each day still feels connected to what you believe in.

Here's how it works:

1   Take a blank page and write down your five core values—the ones you want your leadership and life to reflect most clearly.

2   Next to each, write a few examples of how you've demonstrated that value in the past month.

3   Honestly note where you may have compromised or neglected it—perhaps unintentionally.

4   Circle the one that feels most out of sync right now.

5   Ask yourself, 'What's one small adjustment I could make this week to realign this value with how I'm showing up?'

This isn't about judgement, it's about awareness. The closer our actions mirror our values, the steadier our confidence becomes—and the more trust we build in those around us.

Reflection Exercise
The Decision Debrief

LEADERSHIP IS DEFINED as much by our decisions as by our results. Yet we rarely pause to unpack how those choices were made. This reflection helps you turn hindsight into insight by providing a simple debrief that strengthens your decision-making over time.

Here's how it works:

1   Think of one decision from the past few months that still lingers in your mind: big or small, successful or not.

2   Divide a page into three columns:

- *The context.* What was happening at the time? Who was involved?
- *The choice I made.* What did I decide, and why?
- *What I learnt.* What insights or patterns do I see now?

3   As you write, resist the urge to judge yourself. Instead, look for themes. What influenced you most: logic, instinct, fear or values?

4   End by asking, 'If faced with this again, what would I do the same, and what would I do differently?'

This is not a post-mortem, it's a mirror. Over time, it helps you understand not just what you decided, but who you were when you decided it.

Reflection Exercise
The Trust Ledger

TRUST IS THE quiet currency of leadership. It fuels collaboration, accelerates progress and steadies teams through uncertainty. Yet it's easy to assume it's there without consciously tending to it. This reflection helps you see trust as something living: built, eroded and rebuilt through daily choices.

Here's how it works:

1   Draw two columns:

    - *Where I need to extend more trust*
    - *Where I need to strengthen being trusted*

2   Under the first column, list situations or people where you may be holding back: delegating half-heartedly, double-checking or hesitating to empower.

3   Under the second column, list where others might be uncertain about your reliability or follow-through. Be honest—where might you have unintentionally weakened confidence?

4   For each, write one small action that could rebuild or reinforce trust—a conversation, a commitment, a promise kept.

Trust doesn't grow through grand gestures. It builds quietly in consistently showing up, following through and giving others space to do the same.

Reflection Exercise
The Pause Plan

LEADERS OFTEN WAIT for exhaustion to force rest. But recovery shouldn't be a reaction, it should be a rhythm. This reflection helps you design moments of stillness with intention before the burnout, not after.

Here's how it works:

1   Look ahead at your next ninety days.

2   Mark three intentional pauses: one small (a daily ritual), one medium (a day or weekend) and one large (a break, trip or creative reset).

3   Next to each, write how you'll use that time: rest, reflection, connection or simply doing nothing.

4   Ask yourself, 'What needs to happen now so that these pauses actually hold?' It might be blocking the time, setting boundaries or communicating expectations early.

You don't have to earn rest. Protecting your energy is not indulgence, it's stewardship. When you lead from a place of rest rather than depletion, everyone around you feels the difference.

Reflection Exercise
The Feedback Mirror

FEEDBACK OFTEN LANDS like a verdict. But at its best, it's a reflection. This exercise helps you turn even the hardest feedback into something useful; not a bruise to carry, but a lesson to integrate.

Here's how it works:

1   Choose one piece of feedback—formal or informal, recent or recurring—that has stayed with you.

2   On a new page, write three headers:

   - *What it says*—the words or message itself.
   - *What it stirs in me*—your honest emotional reaction.
   - *What it shows me about myself*—the truth or opportunity beneath it.

3   Reflect: What part of this feedback feels fair? What part might be distorted by perception? What part holds a gift for growth?

4   Then, write one tangible shift—in communication, behaviour, or mindset—that would turn that insight into action.

Feedback becomes wisdom only when we pause long enough to see ourselves within it.

About
the Author

WENDY WALKER is a marketing leader, creative advocate and thoughtful voice on what it really takes to lead with heart. For more than two decades, she has shaped brands and cultures across industries and continents, guiding teams through growth, transformation and creative reinvention.

She believes leadership is not about titles or power, but about the impact we have on others—and the energy we leave behind long after we've moved on.

Wendy's career has spanned senior marketing roles at global, regional and startup levels, always anchored in the conviction that creativity and clarity can drive both impact and integrity. Beyond the corporate world, she has played a significant role in shaping the industry as Founder and President of the International Advertising Association (IAA) Singapore chapter, Global Board Member of the IAA and former Chair of The Marketing Society in Singapore, where she was awarded the title of Fellow. In 2025, she served as Global Jury President for the Creative B2B category at the Cannes Lions International Festival of Creativity, leading discussions that celebrated bold, transformative work on the global stage.

Between Flights is Wendy's first published collection—born from the quiet moments in airports, between flights, where reflection found room to land. These essays offer an honest look at leadership as it's really lived: imperfect, human, and deeply connected to the spaces between ambition and authenticity.

When she's not writing or speaking about leadership and creativity, Wendy finds her own grounding in music, travel and the simple joys of life with her teenage son.

She hopes this book serves as a companion—a quiet space to land for anyone navigating the complexities of leadership and life.

www.ingramcontent.com/pod-product-compliance
Lightning Source LLC
Chambersburg PA
CBHW030503210326
41597CB00013B/775

9781998528745